creative ESSENTIALS

Also by Farah Abushwesha

ROCLIFFE NOTES
A Professional Approach For Screenwriters and Writer-Directors

FARAH ABUSHWESHA

ROCLIFFE NOTES

A GUIDE TO LOW-BUDGET FILMMAKING

creative ESSENTIALS

First published in 2019 by Kamera Books,
an imprint of Oldcastle Books
Harpenden, UK
kamerabooks.com

Copyright © Farah Abushwesha 2019
Series Editor: Hannah Patterson
Editor: Anne Hudson

978-1-84344-914-0 (Print)
978-1-84344-915-7 (epub)

Typeset by Elsa Mathern in DIN and Univers 9 pt
Printed in Great Britain by Clays Ltd, Elcograf, S.p.A.

CONTENTS

CONTRIBUTORS

ADO YOSHIZAKI: Producer, Co-owner NDF International (*City of Tiny Lights, Last Passenger*)

AISLINN CLARKE: Writer, Director (*The Devil's Doorway*)

ANDREA HARKIN: Writer, Director (*Come Home, The Party, The Trial of Christine Keeler*)

DREW JONES: Visual Effects Producer (*Top Boy, Beast*)

ANDREW NERGER: Head of Sales at The Movie Partnership

ANNA GRIFFIN: Producer (*Calibre, The Lilting*)

ANNE LAURILA: Producer, Finnish Film Commission

ASIF KAPADIA: Director (*The Warrior, Senna, Amy*)

BEN BLAINE: Director (*Nina Forever*)

BENNETT MCGHEE: Producer (*VS, Bo66y*)

BRIAN O'SHEA: CEO of The Exchange

CAMILLE GATIN: Producer (*The Girl with All the Gifts, Shadow Dancer*)

CARISSA BUFFEL & KEVIN MATUSOW: CEOs of Traveling Picture Show Company

CHARLES GANT: Film Journalist

CHRISTINE HARTLAND: Producer (*WMD, Containment*)

CLAIRE FREEMAN: Music Supervisor (*The Theory of Everything, City of Tiny Lights*)

CLARE CREAN: Sales & Marketing Consultant

11

CONOR BARRY: Producer (*Mammal, Pilgrimage, You're Ugly Too*)

DANNY HUSTON: Director, Actor (*The Last Photograph, Wonder Woman, Ivansxtc*)

DESTINY EKARAGHA: Director (*A Proposal, Gone Too Far*)

DOMINIC BUCHANAN: Producer (*Gimme the Loot, Lilting, King Jack*)

EMILY MORGAN: Producer (*I Am Not a Witch, Make Up*)

FODHLA CRONIN O'REILLY: Producer (*Lady Macbeth, Head Over Heels, My Generation, Ammonite*)

GEOFFREY AREND: Actor, Director (*500 Days of Summer, Madam Secretary*)

GRAINNE HUMPHREYS: Director of Dublin International Film Festival

HELEN SIMMONS: Producer (*Chubby Funny, Ilkley*)

HILARY DAVIS: Sales & Marketing Consultant

IAN BONHÔTE: Writer, Director, Producer (*McQueen, Alleycats*)

JAMES KNOX: Entertainment Publicist

JOHN MADDEN: Director (*Shakespeare in Love, The Best Exotic Marigold Hotel, Miss Sloane*)

JONNY PATERSON: Producer (*Halfway*)

KRISTEN O'BRIEN: Freelance Entertainment Publicist

LAURENT BOYE: CEO at Jazo PR

LINDSAY CAMPBELL: Producer (*One Million Dubliners, Handy, Strange Occurrences In A Small Irish Village*)

MANON ARDISSON: Producer (*God's Own Country*)

MARNIE PAXTON-HARRIS: Director, Script Supervisor

MASOUD AMRALLA AL ALI: Artistic Director of Dubai International Film Festival

MAXINE PEAKE: Actress, Writer, Director

NICK THURLOW: Producer (*Moonlight, The Kid*)

PAUL SNG: Producer, Director (*Dispossession: The Great Social Housing Swindle, Sleaford Mods: Invisible Britain*)

PETER PEDRERO: Stunt Coordinator (*Harry Potter and the Deathly Hallows, Avengers: Age of Ultron*)

PETER SMYTH: Producer (*Lady Macbeth, Containment*)

RAY PANTHAKI: Actor, Writer, Director (*Colette, Convenience*)

RORY DUNGAN: Producer (*The Cured*)

SALLY EL HOSAINI: Director (*My Brother The Devil, Babylon*)

SARAH ARNOTT: Sales & Marketing Consultant

SARAH BROCKLEHURST: Producer (*Black Pond, Animals*)

SARAH GAVRON: Director (*Suffragette, Brick Lane*)

SAUL DIBB: Writer, Director (*The Duchess, Bullet Boy*)

SEAN BAKER: Writer, Director (*The Florida Project, Tangerine, Starlet*)

SHANNON THOMPSON: Make-Up Designer (*Irreplaceable You, Fast Colour*)

SHARON BIALY: Casting Director (*Irreplaceable You, The Handmaid's Tale*)

SHIRLEY HENDERSON: Actor (*Stan & Ollie, The ABC Murders,* Harry Potter films)

STEPHANIE LAING: Director, Producer (*Irreplaceable You, Veep*)

TINA GHARAVI: Director (*I Am Nasrine*)

VERITY WISLOCKI: Producer, Post-production Supervisor, Wislocki Films (*The Killing of a Sacred Deer, The Imitation Game*)

WENDY MITCHELL: Contributing Editor Screen International, Film Festivals Aficionado

WHITNEY ANNE ADAMS: Costume Designer (*Irreplaceable You, Piercing*)

**Dedicated to the memory of screenwriter
Eoin Rogers 1977-2017 with stories still to tell,
he ceaselessly gave up his time to support and
encourage other filmmakers.**

INTRODUCTION

So you want to make a low-budget film? You've seen people do it, you've got a story to tell – it must be achievable! But then you think about the nitty-gritty: turning your brilliant idea into a fully fleshed-out script, casting it, financing it, figuring out the length, the style, the audience, the budget... and suddenly, it can feel very unachievable. Think of this book as a guide to help you know that yes, it can be done.

This book is for those embarking on making a short or a feature – whether you're a director, writer, actor, producer or doing everything yourself. It is a demystification – from understanding the rudiments of budgeting and scheduling to creating a finance plan. This is not an exact or comprehensive guide; it is the things I needed to know or have been asked the most.

A film made for a low or micro-budget means you're forced to think about solutions creatively, even more creatively than if you had the biggest budget in Hollywood – that's the key to low-budget filmmaking. The process will be tough and the rewards may feel far away, but your focus as a filmmaker is to make the best film you can possibly make. Expect the unexpected and that mistakes will happen, and remember your priority isn't what festival or platform you screen on, but to make the best possible version of your film. Don't make yourself a prisoner of the things you get wrong. As Oscar Wilde said, experience is the name everyone gives to their mistakes. Give yourself permission to make something, to fail or succeed at it, and then do it again. Don't listen to the voice in your head telling you 'you can't', or those you think may ridicule you for aspiring to something more. Nothing beats the experience of doing it yourself.

I cut my producing teeth by making several shorts. I worked as a production coordinator on *The Scouting Book for Boys* with Tom Harper, Jack Thorne and Ivana Mackinnon. On that film, I met many great people who I continue to collaborate with today. My first feature as a producer was *Pressure*. On that film Danny Huston asked me to be a producer on *The Last Photograph*. I made a Screen Ireland signatures short, *The Party*, with Andrea Harkin and Conor MacNeill, which was nominated for a BAFTA and a European Film Award. Through Rocliffe New Writing Competition I met Stephanie Laing, made comedy content for her comedy platform PYPO, and later produced her directorial debut, Netflix Original *Irreplaceable You*.

My immense gratitude to those who painstakingly read, reread, consulted and advised – Wendy Mitchell, Emily Morgan, Ed Cripps, Verity Wislocki, Helen Simmons, Catherine Freeman, Aiman Aliff and Christos Michaels for their thoughts on early drafts of this. Thank you too to the generosity of my fellow filmmakers who contributed their experiences so honestly.

DISCLAIMER

The copyright and samples in this book are owned and retained by the originator of the work. This work has been created for your general information only. The owner, the author of this book and the publishers cannot therefore be held responsible for any losses or claims howsoever arising from any use or reproduction. Nothing in this book should be construed as legal advice. The information provided is not a substitute for consulting with an experienced entertainment lawyer, film practitioners, or receiving counsel based on the facts and circumstances of a particular transaction. Furthermore, case law and statutes and European and international law and industry practice are subject to change, and differ from country to country.

This book is about good practice.

01

THE LADDER

Each project has its own unique requirements, and these will give you a unique and first-hand insight into the things that work for those making films (extraordinary ones) at lower-budget levels. Filmmaking is a journey – there are highs and lows. Enjoy the highs for they are few and far between. You can't predict the outcome but you can learn from the process and meet collaborators doing it.

There are different kinds of filmmakers at different levels. There's always something to be learned from everyone you meet, both higher up and lower down.

LEVEL: FIRST-TIMER/NEWBIE (GREAT PLACE TO BE)

IS THIS YOU: Never made a film, never read a script but want to make something to see how it works and fancy giving it a go.

EXPERIENCE: Know little about equipment, have no money but plenty of willing friends and family who will help out.

AUDIENCE: Cast, crew, friends and family – maybe festivals if you submit.

WHERE TO START: Read shorts, read about writing shorts, write a script, do a short course to see how it works, make a film on a phone.

LEVEL: HAVE SOME EXPERIENCE

IS THIS YOU: Made one or two shorts, worked in film, done a few courses.

EXPERIENCE: Know a bit about equipment, got some contacts in the industry and got a little money. Know the technical side and feel a bit more prepped in terms of what you have to do and what to expect. More confident about what can be done.

AUDIENCE: Cast, crew, friends, family, industry and festival circuit.

WHERE TO START: Get feedback on the script, call in favours from industry contacts, apply to funding schemes.

LEVEL: SEMI-PROFESSIONAL

IS THIS YOU: Made several shorts including award-winners, have an agent, need a producer and a feature film.

EXPERIENCE: Ready to make a feature, have good contacts in the industry, confident in ability and know what matters on a set.

AUDIENCE: Potential strong launch at festival with good reviews and potential for distribution.

WHERE TO START: Make the script the best it can be, talk with sales agents and work with experienced DoPs and production designers to prep.

ASK FOR ADVICE

The best way to get started is to ask for advice from those who have experience. They won't have all the answers but they may tell you how they would have done things differently.

Prepare for that meeting and make sure all parties are aware of the purpose of it. Send a short, but sweet, email asking to meet for a coffee for advice on a particular topic. If the person you ask can't help, they may be able to direct you to someone who can.

Most people will be happy to share their pearls of wisdom on how they got into the industry. The most common questions are about how to find the money, feedback, careers, budgets, who to collaborate with, how to get a script to work and then get it made. Probably where to find funding is the most-asked question before 'Will you read my script?'. Apart from the usual suspects like funding bodies, they may offer practical help such as recommendations for crew and producers.

There's a difference between asking for advice and asking someone to give you their expertise for free. Some expertise will come with a small fee – a professional script report, a budget, a schedule. Before you complain, this is the price of business. Come to expect this.

Be honest about the advice you are looking for. You won't be the first and certainly not the last to ask for help and, as you make your way up the ladder, it is expected. Most of us will send the ladder back down, but make a favourable impression and come prepared.

ROCLIFFE NOTES on...

MEETING FOR ADVICE

- Get a notebook and a pen or pencil. Take it with you everywhere and make notes.

- There is a lot of information on the web.

- Prepare a list of questions to ask at meetings on what you've read or learnt – although avoid conspiracy theories.

- Before sending someone a script to read or a film to watch – ask! Don't assume people have the time and don't be cross if they haven't.

- Spend the time listening to the experienced person, not talking about what **you** want to do or trying to compete with them – they've got the years/credits.

- Be wary of myths of people stealing ideas – there are less sharks and most people are willing to help and have integrity, but protect your work. Email it. Watermark it. Keep track of who you tell it to. Ideas are in the ether – use them or lose them.

- Ask people how they got started or have seen other people break in.

- Enjoy the company of the person you are meeting and don't expect to learn how to make a film in an hour – there's no fast or magic answer.

- Ask people to connect you with others in the industry. If getting a quote from a camera house, ask if they can recommend a DoP – make connections. Someone may pass on your contact details even if they don't give you a direct contact.

- When looking for a producer or writer, look at recent graduates from film schools, award-winning films, go to film festivals, watch short films and read the credits, go on training schemes – connect.

- Write to literary agents to ask for recommendations but send them a short brief of what you are looking for – is it a short or feature?

- Check the recent funding rounds from national funding bodies – who is on their watch list?

- Go on short courses or initiatives – Screen Training Ireland and ScreenSkills, for example.

- Keep all your questions to a single email. Sending question after question clogs up an inbox and is disrespectful.

SHORTS

For many of us, working on shorts gives us some experience. There has been such a change in recent years with camera phones and the internet that shorts and short-form content are now easy to produce for anyone wishing to do so.

Shorts can be great films. They are an amazing way to learn and understand the different crafts behind the technical arts such as editing, camera, sound and lighting.

They can take you on journeys to film festivals and a network of new talent. What a short can do is prove what you are capable of and work as a showreel of work you have done.

While a short provides an absolutely brilliant learning curve, it doesn't automatically make you a feature-filmmaker. Where a short differs from a feature is that a story told in ten minutes is not necessarily one that can be stretched out to 90 minutes. The structure is different. Shorts don't usually make their money back. They will generate interest, but not necessarily. You need to commit time and money and they take a lot of effort to set up.

Short films allow you the space to learn and lessons to be learned, including multitasking as an individual and as a team. You will discover that what you need to know more than anything is how a set works, physically and mentally.

Some newer producers and directors think it's about control, which it is, but mostly it's about handling responsibility and communication. The biggest responsibility when dealing with actors, crew, budgets and other aspects of a production is staying calm. A stressed-out producer or director means everyone else will be stressed-out too. The biggest lesson you need to learn when making shorts is how to remain calm and to calm the people around you.

These skills are not necessarily innate. You have to learn to steer yourself and develop the confidence to share your vision or communicate your team's vision, while at all times being financially responsible. It can be overwhelming, but the overriding rule of filmmaking is that nothing is unachievable. There is always a way round a problem and you can always find a solution while keeping things in perspective.

Ask yourself why you want to make this film and what you want from it. What do you want this film to do? Why do you want to tell this story?

THE VALUE OF SHORTS

Shorts are fantastic because, in a short time, you learn to handle the all-encompassing responsibilities of managing a crew, cast, finances, creativity and, above all, delivering a film. I actually believe you have more creative control on a short than on a feature and it's a wonderful way to grow and learn.

RORY DUNGAN: We're lucky in Ireland that there exists a variety of soft funds for making short films (Filmbase, Galway Film Centre, Cork Film Centre). We accessed as many of them as we could. They were always highly competitive so many projects never quite made it, but, thankfully for us, a lot of them did. This allowed us then to start making shorts with Screen Ireland and start getting our feature films developed through funding with them.

FODHLA CRONIN O'REILLY: Will [Oldroyd] and I shot a teaser and it was good to see how he was on set and for us to get to know how the other worked. It built trust and a shorthand.

CONOR BARRY: Shorts are a proof of your ability to hold responsibility and a remit, but also, as a writer/director or producer, you're involved with a particular style of filmmaking, not a copy of other things. You should be able to go 'that's what I'm about'. It's a calling card in terms of the tone or style.

SARAH GAVRON: You have to show you can direct in order get a directing job. Short films are a great way, or commercials or theatre – whatever it is that shows your work as a director. I made nine short films and it was with the ninth short that I had my break – it won some awards, got me an agent and meetings with film companies and broadcasters. I made that short while at the National Film and TV School – having fellow students, equipment and expert guidance on hand helped enormously.

TINA GHARAVI: Shorts are great – they are such an important part of building your storytelling confidence and testing yourself.

DESTINY EKARAGHA: Short-film funding schemes helped to jumpstart my career. Southern Exposure, a borough fund, funded *Tight Jeans*. *The Park* was funded by Film London. The funding and support I got from each of them enabled me to make the films exactly as I intended and for that I will always be grateful.

SALLY EL HOSAINI: I made a 60-second short, then another longer short film. I then tried to make some much more ambitious short films but never got the funding together. The only reason I made shorts later in my career was because I kept getting told that you have to make shorts to show what you can do in order to make a feature. So, for me, short films were always a means to an end.

WHAT ARE SHORTS?

I can't remember who first said it but I've never forgotten the advice to think of shorts as visual poems building atmosphere and tone.

Film is a subjective medium. We all know what we like and don't like. We can be looking at the same film and it will engage us differently. There are no rules, and then, on the other hand, there is nothing but the rules: rules of genre, etiquette, form and expectation.

Short film and form is exploding, not only in Ireland and the UK but also globally. Although with the changing economic climate there are fewer funding opportunities for short-film schemes than a few years ago, in the rest of the world a whole new generation of filmmakers from Eastern Europe, Asia and the Middle East are finding their filmmaking voices. Adverts want short-form stories, editorial wants stories, and we even have stories on Snapchat and can put videos on Instagram.

Add to this digital technology, and the fact that some celebrated short films were actually conceived, made and produced in someone's bedroom, and you can see why there are so many short films saturating the marketplace. For your short film to be noticed you really have to make something that's unique, visionary and pleasing to an audience.

Watching shorts is essential for filmmakers. Try to watch as many as you can. Creative inspiration comes from many sources and the best way to learn what works is by watching where others fail. Too few aspiring filmmakers watch shorts. You also have to care passionately about the story because it is a time-consuming labour of love.

ROCLIFFE NOTES on...
ASSESSING SHORT FILMS

Watch short films to see what kind of shorts work for you. Constantly be asking questions – why, what, when, who and where? The great thing about shorts and short-film scripts is that they can be read/watched, assessed and dissected quickly:

- What does it make you think of?
- Can you sum it up in one line?
- What genre is it?
- What do you think the starting point (inspiration) for the writer was or what do you think the writer was trying to say with it?
- Does the story have a beginning, middle and end?
- Did the ending work for you?
- Does the script excite you or bore you?
- What do you find frustrating or irritating about this script?
- What does it say to you?

- How successfully is the writer building character?
- Are they trying to tell too big a story that isn't appropriate for the length?
- How does the writer deal with time?
- Does it resonate with you after you've read/watched it?
- Is there an image that sticks in your mind?
- Ask questions – why, what, where, when and how

FUNDING A SHORT FILM

There really are only a few possible sources of finance for a short:

- New talent film funds – Screen Ireland, BFI (see SOFT MONEY SOURCES)
- Regional funds – Film London, Northern Ireland Screen, FilmBase Ireland, etc. (see SOFT MONEY SOURCES)
- Crowdfunding
- Pay for it yourself
- Short film competitions from branded content schemes – Jameson Short Film, MoFilm and Bombay Sapphire (which exist at time of print)
- Bank of Mum and Dad – never underestimate the power of love. Also, friends and family tend to offer better interest rates than credit cards and banking institutions

SHORT-FILM PRODUCTION SCHEDULE

The prep, production and post-production of a short film are similar to that of a feature, just shorter.

Production of a short film involves many different things and the first thing to do is create a summary schedule of key activities from pre-production, production and post-production – outlining each phase and estimated dates for delivering your project.

ROCLIFFE NOTES on...
SHORT-FILM PRODUCTION

- Decide how you are going to fund it. There are three options – a new talent initiative, crowdfunding or self-funding.
- Set a shoot date or time to shoot – this can be determined by cast, location or DoP availability.
- Prep time is your best friend.
- Minimise locations and logistics.
- Decide what you are going to shoot it on.
- Scout locations.
- Get your production insurance.
- Meet with key crew – production design, costume, make-up, etc.

SAMPLE SHORT-FILM PRODUCTION SCHEDULE

Short film, shot on digital with four cast members on location. The budget is £9,000. Shoot is one day exterior and three days of interior.

It has been agreed:

- Prep – 5 weeks
- Shoot – 4 days
- Edit – 10 days
- Post-production – 4 weeks

PRODUCTION SCHEDULE – SHORT-FILM SAMPLE

Activity	Tasks
PRE-PRODUCTION	
Week – 5 (Shoot week minus 5)	Casting the leads Location scouting Post-production deals Contact agents for HoDs Insurance
Week – 4	Meeting with HoDs Director of Cinematography Production Designer Costume Designer Sound Recordist Visit locations Contact catering companies
Week – 3	Discuss with HoDs crew and equipment requirements Get quotes Contact suppliers and crew Advertise for crew
Week – 2	Location tech recce with DoP, Art, Sound Book equipment
Week – 1	Check with each department for their needs Create contracts, call sheets and schedules
PRODUCTION	
Day 1	Exterior
Day 2	Interior
Day 3	Interior
Day 4	Interior
POST-PRODUCTION	
Edit Day 1	Ingest media and sort into scenes and takes
Edit Day 2	Assembly Edit

Activity	Tasks
Edit Day 3	Editing and first assembly sent to producers and execs for feedback
Edit Day 4	EDIT – send first assembly to producers and execs for feedback
Edit Days 5–7	EDIT – get notes and cut film
	Get feedback on cut
	Show cuts to other filmmakers
	Play around with their feedback
Edit Day 8	Implement changes
Post Day	Visual effects/Special effects, Music cues
Edit Days 9–10	Drop in VFX/SFX/Music to film – may need minor frame changes
	Lock film and do playouts – editor create the EDL (edit decision list)
	NOTE: If you can afford more time in the edit then go for it
1–2 Days	Foley, AD, Pre-mix
1–2 Days	Conform and grade
	Track lay

ROCLIFFE NOTES on...

SHORT-FILM SHOTS

- Consider scheduling your shoot over a weekend when you stand a better chance of getting more experienced crew and cast.

- It's hard to remember everything and it's your first time, so prepare a storyboard, shot list and keep a check list.

- Check the weather forecast for exterior scenes and try to schedule them first if possible.

- Storyboard action or visual scenes.

- Director and DoP prepare a shot list and circulate to Camera Department and 1st AD. Even if you structure the scene as it would play in the edit, always go for a single shot and master of each scene (capturing the scene in one shot).

- Break down how long you are going to spend on each scene by shot and time spent on each.

Basic shot list includes:

- Single shot of the entire scene

- Single on each of the characters speaking

- Shot by shot in the order of the edit for an action/visual sequence – usually storyboarded

- Coverage or reaction shots on characters

••

Short film, shot on digital with four cast members on location. The budget is £9,000. Shoot is one day exterior and three days of interior.

▶ **See Sample Short-Film Budget – £9,000 in the Appendix**

If you have little or no money and can just about cover some insurance and basic needs and decided:

- Prep – 1 week
- Shoot – 1 day
- Edit – 4 days
- Post-production – 2 days

▶ **See Sample Short-Film Budget – £850 in the Appendix**

03

DEVELOPING AND PACKAGING A MOVIE

A MOVIE

Filmmaking is a non-exact science and you need to prepare. I've compared it to crawling uphill on your knees. When you get to the top, regardless of what the views are like – cloudy or clear – take pride in what you've achieved in getting there. There are many rewards to be had – creative, collaborative and sometimes financial.

BENNETT MCGHEE: Be prepared to wait and be patient, but also to push at the right time. In my early days all I needed was a mobile phone and a laptop and a source of power so London was my office. When things grew a desk became necessary but I've resisted as long as possible and saved a lot of money. Be prepared to get emotional at the right time and hold your nerve at all other times. Be prepared to put in the hours, weeks, months, years. It will almost certainly not happen overnight. I'm not sure there's one best route into producing but certainly working for producers you admire and who are willing to nurture you, as I was fortunate enough to do, was an incredibly important part of my route to producing. There's a tipping point where the pressure starts to mount. After years in development waiting on people to read and say yes, then the finance and cast are in place and it becomes an ever-increasing wave of business, legal, logistics, politics and crisis management that you're constantly trying to ride to avoid a wipe-out.

People who are about to embark on making a micro- or low-budget feature think the journey is about success and failure and have one or two scenarios in their heads.

The Journey of a Movie

An idea → A script → Get the money → Shoot the movie → Edit the movie → Festival premiere → Cinema → Box-office hit → Awards → Make lots of money → An idea

or

The Journey of a Movie

An idea → A script → Get the money → Shoot the movie → Edit the movie → Cast and crew screening → Nothing happens → Broke/Broken filmmaker

33

HELEN SIMMONS: If you're determined to be a filmmaker and know it's your calling, the only thing to do is get on and do it. And that means staying strong and ignoring the many naysayers you'll meet along the way. There will be many doubters, many who don't understand, many who think they know best and even some who are simply jealous that perhaps they didn't take the risk you've decided to take and now it's too late. You will probably be told you're doing the wrong thing, or that perhaps you should take that runner job for another year, or work for someone else for another five, and did you know you're never going to make any money and should probably be an accountant/lawyer/teacher/[insert stable job here]? A lot of what makes someone successful in a business like this is grit and perseverance. Don't take no for an answer. Don't settle – for a mediocre script or film or career. And don't give up on yourself. It's a long road and there will most definitely be times when you want to quit. But then you have a cry or a moan and you dust yourself off and keep going. If anything, I think that's the number-one quality common to almost every filmmaker I've ever met. They just keep going.

Bennett and Helen sum up so well the different routes. A film may do well on the festival circuit and not make its money back and yet be well-received critically. It may even skip some of these routes along the way and go straight on to a platform as we did with *Irreplaceable You*. The film was released as a Netflix Original in 2018.

What you want to happen is for the film to be seen by the biggest audience possible and for it to make its money back or do its backers proud. Make something that shows you are worth investing in. Netflix has enabled us to make the investors' money back and get seen by the widest audience. My experience of them was great and very transparent. For us it was the best scenario we could have hoped for.

RAY PANTHAKI: In amidst all the anxiety that comes with making a film, remind yourself to enjoy it.

The Journey of a Movie

An idea

A script

Get the money

Shoot the movie

Edit/post/ deliver film

A-List festival premiere

Festival circuit & positive reviews

Sales & theatrical/online release

Makes its money back

. . . .

ROCLIFFE NOTES on...

WHAT A FILM IS

- A film is a series of moving images and sound/music, which tell a story.

- A film is a product, a commodity that can be sold to make money for its investors.

- A feature needs to be a minimum of 71 minutes long.

- A film is made for an audience – so know who your audience is.

- A film conforms to a genre – comedy, horror, thriller and drama.

- A film has a world, a location, characters, emotion and a problem/ dilemma or central conflict to overcome.

- A film can be summed up in one line or 25 words.

- A film is rarely, if ever, unique – it can be original but it usually has similarities with a story told before.

- A film is made by a series of people in collaboration – no one person can take credit for all the work.

....

KEEP THE SCRIPT WITHIN A LOW OR MICRO-BUDGET

A film begins with an idea that becomes a script. My last book dealt with scripts and screenplays. The focus of this book is more on the practical side of production. That said, there are quintessential ways to write a film that can be made for a lower budget without rehashing what has been done before.

A budget decides everything. An important question to ask is whether the budget is a good match for the film, i.e. can this film be done this way?

Some of the films made on low or micro-budgets are creatively inspiring. They work because they are made out of necessity, a deep-rooted desire and determination to tell the story. With low-budget films the only limitation is the amount of money you can raise to make the film happen. Recent films such as *Lady Macbeth* prove that. That doesn't mean you lose the story. In fact, DON'T LOSE THE STORY because you will not have the perfect budget to shoot it. The script will carry the film from start to finish and you are the creator of that world, so think of it as a challenge and be creative.

There are conventions to low-budget filmmaking that we all need to consider when writing a film. You'll have to compromise in the course of making the film, but that's the nature of collaboration.

We can all think of first films that were made on a shoestring and learn from them. The French New Wave made iconic auteurs of Godard, Truffaut, Demy and Rivette, and grew out of an economic necessity that gave birth to an era of filmmaking that allowed directors the freedom to explore style and story in their own way. The French New Wave began in the late 1950s and continued through the 1960s. The filmmakers shot films dealing with very contemporary political and social issues on location, and experimented with editing

A ROUGH GUIDE TO BUDGETS

Shorts can be from £5 to £50,000 (sometimes more)
Micro-budget is up to £150,000*
Ultra-low-budget is up to £500,000*
Low-budget is up to £1,300,000*

*Opinions differ depending on who you're talking to and the country in which they are based. Stephen Follows, in 2014, surveyed 542 industry professionals about what classified as a micro-budget and found the average maximum to be £243,000.

Source: https://stephenfollows.com/average-budget-low-micro-budget-film

and cinematography as part of a narrative style. In documentary style, they used portable equipment and required little or no setup time.

The recent wave of films made for low or micro-budgets in the UK and Ireland are similar to the French New Wave – they have allowed filmmakers to create a space for their own voices without having the pressure of a studio system behind them. Recent production schemes such as Catalyst in Ireland, Microwave and iFeatures support filmmakers in this way by providing the finance and support to allow a new generation of filmmakers to explore creatively.

As with all films, there has to be a truth, a fundamental truth, at the heart of each story you are going to tell.

Without a doubt, shorts and films made for low or micro-budgets have paved the way for many familiar names today – for example, Paul King, Sean Baker, Christopher Nolan, Joe Cornish, Andrea Arnold, Ben Wheatley, Clio Barnard, Gareth Edwards, Eran Creevy and Catherine Hardwicke.

Take a look at Jason Blum's Blumhouse Productions, whose films include *Paranormal Activity*, *Whiplash* and *Get Out*, and their model of making low-budget films. In his own words, his method for making movies as economically as possible begins with looking for films he likes and then assessing if they can be done on a low budget –

not looking for low-budget films to make. His rules are simple: limit the number of speaking parts; limit the locations; pay the actors the minimum but offer a percentage; and never break the budget – meaning don't throw money at a problem, solve it creatively. He was quoted on IMDb as advising aspiring filmmakers to 'raise whatever you can and shoot whatever you can for whatever amount'.

Regardless of the budget, the script is the cheapest thing to fix. It needs to have characters, plot, a clear premise, a genre, locations, and it has to be resourceful and innovative.

The Blair Witch Project really started a found-footage phenomenon. It was unconventional and audiences went in their droves. No one wants to see a rehash of what exists. Do it better and put an original spin on it. Tell it your way, not someone else's. Bring your voice to the table.

Sometimes it's worth looking at a film as having a specific set of rules and sticking to them. I'm not suggesting this is the only way to do it, but these are a few tried and tested conventions which may drive you to be creatively unconventional with a budget.

ROCLIFFE NOTES on...
CREATIVE SOLUTIONS

- The length of the script is relevant – you have less time to shoot so the shorter the script the more time you have to shoot the story. Try and stick to between 75 and 90 pages.

- There's nothing to say you can't set it on a spaceship, but that may be the only location other than a beach or desert for some exteriors.

- Public spaces such as airports, train stations and Buckingham Palace are hard to control and can be pricey, along with heavy set-builds such as airplane interiors. Instead, create a corridor with airport signs near a window and use stock footage to establish where it is.

- It's cheaper to shoot during the day than at night. Exterior nighttime scenes need lighting.

- Casting is crucial – limit the number of cast and extras. Have strong characters that are well written and well thought out. Too often the underwritten characters are the female roles.

- Driving sequences and stunts are expensive and time-consuming. Have someone pull up in the car or remove the headrests and film characters from behind as they speak inside the vehicle.

- Rain – can they come in wet? You can't film rain; it isn't visible on-screen and you need special equipment. Anything with water (wet downs, underwater) costs money!

- Got a chase sequence? Have the actors run or being chased. You won't need special equipment and it can be shot quickly.

- Blood, guts, guns and explosions – blood travelling, moving and splattering involves special-effects teams and a lot of clever design. Armourers are needed with guns, particularly in the open air, or you could be arrested. You must have an armourer if a gun fires. With explosions you need professional special-effects teams and a nurse standing by. If you're inside and a gun isn't real or doesn't fire, you're okay.

- Need to film at a concert? Get in touch with up-and-coming bands and ask if you can film their gig and feature their song? They retain the rights to their music and are promoted in a film.

DIRECTOR AND PRODUCER MEET

I've been fortunate enough to get to work with some great directors this way. Susan Jacobson and I met through a short-film funding scheme run by the then UKFC (now BFI).

Making that crucial connection – with your director or producer – may feel impossible. How will I find them or even know they exist? How do I reach out? Often, it's a combination of determined networking, and a sort of right place, right time fortuitousness. With the directors I've worked with, it's been a real mixture. Some I met at formal networking events – funding schemes, film festivals such as Cannes, at the Rocliffe Showcase – and others informally. One director I met on set and we got along so well we decided to work together; another was introduced to me by her sister; another at a birthday party! You never know where you might make that connection and hit it off. If you do, congratulations, you've found a good match. Now you just have to work out if you want to make the same film.

Sometimes you start out collaborating with someone but, along the way, one of you realises it isn't a great pairing. And it's not that anyone is to blame – it's just not right for one reason or another. This happens.

AISLINN CLARKE: My producers on *The Devil's Doorway* were looking for a director who would be able to work with improvisation. I have many years' experience as a theatre director, so Ursula Devine at Northern Ireland Screen recommended me and other directors. When I first met the producer, Martin Brennan, the film was a one-page outline. The Magdalene laundries subject matter appealed to me as I have a particular interest in Irish church/state mistreatment of women and I love horror. I said I'd do it, but I was concerned that such a project could be exploitative with the tropes of the possession subgenre, so often there is a major element of female sexual expression being controlled and subdued. Given the similarity there to the intended function of Magdalene laundries I felt we had to tread carefully. There was potentially an opportunity here to make the best sort of horror, something searing and politically relevant. Intelligently and empathetically; using and subverting the tropes of the subgenre in a way that explored the wound left behind by these institutions without exploiting the victims. I laid out my vision for how I would handle such a project and expected never to hear from him again. While many would be tempted to say 'yes' in order to get their first feature-film made, I have enough experience and respect for my own work to be able to say no to things I don't feel are right for me.

It turned out that he liked my very different vision for the film and came back to me to ask if I'd take on the job, and I did.

CAMILLE GATIN: I always seek out shorts that are winning festivals, graduation shorts from film schools or recommendations from agents and meet with the director of those I enjoy,

DOMINIC BUCHANAN: It's hard to find a good producer and there are only a few of us younger producers who've been able to build up a track record with films we've made – that have had some impact in the UK (critically and commercially), as well as premiering at prestige festivals around the world. There is still a lack of support for producers coming up, whether in or out of the system, especially those from diverse backgrounds.

RORY DUNGAN: David [Freyne] and I actually studied film together in college. Being of a similar mindset and 100% determined to make a career of this, we blindly established a production company, soon after college finished, with another film-school friend [Rachel O'Kane]. Two of us are producers, and he's the writer/director. We all continued working in other capacities in paid employment within the industry for several years, gathering experience, while we chipped away at building up a collection of short films through the company, in order to establish ourselves. We've made our first feature film, *The Cured*, so the long journey has been worth it to get to this point!

ADO YOSHIZAKI: Finding the right director for my projects is probably the most important aspect of development so I've taken quite a varied approach. Each project has to be looked at carefully and individually to assess its needs and I tend to separate directors into three categories: inexperienced (first-timers or with one or two films), peers (with some overlap with the first category) and experienced directors (usually well-known). For each category there is a different approach. For new directors, I find that, once every couple of years, it's useful to contact agents and arrange a series of meetings with those who have shown promise and get to know a bit about them and their aims and aspirations. If there is good chemistry and shared tastes then we may end up working together in the future. Once I started to make films, I found that, on occasion, directors would approach me to produce their films. I'm working with a couple of directors now who fall into that category. These directors tend to be peers, i.e. we know each other, or each other's work, and I can either approach them with projects or vice versa. However, as we initiate most of our own projects, the majority of our director attachments are made by making lists of those who would fit the profile of the project and a (sometimes long) process of sending the material and aligning availabilities until there is a happy working partnership in place.

MANON ARDISSON: Francis (writer-director), Jack (producer) and I all met on the same day in February 2014 at a Screen Yorkshire networking event called Triangle. Francis already had an early version of the script he had tried to finance with another producer who wasn't attached anymore, and was looking for a young and hungry producer to come on board. Jack and I really loved his pitch – which felt personal, authentic and new – and we decided to team up to produce it together. I literally emailed Jack 'in union there is strength', and I'm glad he agreed, because producing together was a much better experience than it would have been on my own. What really attracted me about the project was the opportunity to tell a same-sex love story that didn't end up in tragedy – which is often the case in LGBT cinema because of the historical oppression of LGBT people. I felt *God's Own Country* offered a new yet authentic take that I wanted to see on-screen.

JONNY PATERSON: I met Ben [Caird] at a networking event in Los Angeles for British ex-pats right around the time we both moved to the city in 2012. We were the two youngest people there by a mile, so naturally gravitated towards one another and the rest is history!

BEN BLAINE: Our debut feature film, *Nina Forever*, was produced by Cassandra Sigsgaard who we'd first met four years earlier on a talent scheme called Think-Shoot-Distribute, which ran for a week alongside the London Film Festival, hot-housing small groups of filmmakers. Among others in our year were Cass, Tess Morris (writer, *Man Up*) and Andrew Haigh (*Weekend*, *45 Years*). Two years before that Cass had been at the premiere of our Film4/UKFC short film *Hallo Panda*, which she had adored. After getting to know each other properly, we stayed in touch and a year later she optioned a feature-film version of *Hallo Panda*, after she'd found out we'd written it and were doing a reading of it at the BAFTA Rocliffe Showcase and got to have a read for herself. The script requires an entirely animatronic zoo, so the budget was beyond us back then, but working together on the project was a really good way of defining our dynamic. That said, we sort of expected her to disown us when we showed her the script of *Nina Forever*... Luckily, she instantly saw the potential.

CARISSA BUFFEL & KEVIN MATUSOW: We, our team at Traveling Picture Show Company (TPSC), have a few ways of going about the director search. Sometimes it's just research and tracking down directors from work (shorts, features, etc.) that we have seen and liked. Sometimes it's working through reps we know who are fostering up-and-coming talent.

DIRECTOR-PRODUCER WORKING RELATIONSHIP AND PREPARATION

Working on a film is teamwork – a collaboration based on clarity of communication and trust. At the heart of this is the relationship among director, producer and writer. In my last book I focused on the writer and writer-director relationship, and the development of the project. If you've not made a film together before, even a short, that relationship and dynamic will be tested during the financing and prep stages.

The producer-director relationship is key to the film's success or failure. It must be based on principles of transparency and honesty. Effective collaboration, creativity, practical management and communication form the backbone of every successful production. How a project is managed comes from the top down.

The main responsibility of a producer is to deliver a film on time, within budget, creatively, and of the quality and in the style agreed at the point of financing, in collaboration with the director.

The director is responsible, in collaboration with the producer, for all the creative and craft aspects of production. A team will always look to the director to be the driving inspiration behind the project from pre-production through to final grading.

The producer needs to make the director aware of what the **budget** is and how they can make the film they imagine within that budget.

The initial reach-out for **heads of department (HoDs)** and main cast may often fall to the producer, who will cold call talent agents and ask other filmmakers for recommendations. The producer and director should decide together on the HoDs. The director, in consultation with the producer, chooses the key team members such as director of photography (DoP), production designer (PD), 1st assistant director (1st AD), editor (Ed), make-up & hair designer (MUHD), sound recordist (SR), costume designer (CD) and composer. Financiers may ask for HoD approval or consultation, and before offering anyone the job, reference checks should be done on all candidates.

The director and producer will discuss **casting** but it is ultimately the director who will be working closely with the actors and be responsible for delivering the best performances. Financiers may ask for cast approval or consultation.

Production design is discussed by the director, producer and production designer, with the costumes and make-up completing the look of the film.

The director and DoP discuss the **cinematography** by photographing images, talking ideas, watching films together, discussing style and tone.

The director also needs to meet with the **sound recordist** and post **sound design** team. The importance of a good sound recordist is often neglected. Sound, as we will discover later, can catch you out in post, and prove costly if it isn't done well. Is there a song you will need played or cleared in advance – start in prep.

The director and producer should draw up a brief with **location** references of what they are looking for so that when they meet the location manager (LM) they will understand what is wanted. Locations will then be chosen with the input of the location manager, 1st assistant director, director of photography, sound recordist and production designer.

Visual effects (VFX) and **post-production** should be consulted early in prep.

ROCLIFFE NOTES on...

DIRECTOR-PRODUCER
PRE-PREP CONVERSATION

- Find out how the director likes to work and any particular working requirements.

- Create a time frame for prep and script delivery.

- Who have you both got in mind for casting?

- Who is the audience?

- Discuss the budget and be aware of the limitations – this is key to knowing if you are making the same film.

- Share the outline of the whole production schedule from prep to post and final delivery.

- Discuss the time frame and what you are committing – film-making is a long, long game.

- Who do you both have in mind as key crew?

- What are you deciding about the different cuts of the film – when will the director be happy to show you the work? Set benchmarks and deadlines.

- During the prep period, where are you going to work from? Where will the director work? It's not a good idea to work from home if there are distractions.

- Where will the film be edited?

- How are you going to support yourself outside of the production period?

- How much time can you give to the film in the production, post and editing period?

PITCH AND PACKAGE

The key skill of a producer is the ability to multitask and communicate: having the creative vision to drive the film forward and the entrepreneurial skills and energy to raise the money to get it made. A producer develops the work with the writer and director to make a script that attracts talent, and the talent ensures that the money can flow. A director will need to know and describe the kind of film they want to make. And everyone needs to be excited about your project!

ROCLIFFE NOTES on...
THE VERBAL PITCH

- What is your film about?
- What is the potential market?
- How will the film recoup in this market?
- What is the budget range?
- Why are you making the film now?
- What films is it similar to in tone or genre?
- Who are the potential cast? Are they attached?
- Does the screenplay create questions: will she find out the truth? Did he do it? Will they fall in love?
- Has a strong 'need to know' hook been built into the story?
- Add visual reference material to set mood, tone, style, genre.

BASIC FILM OVERVIEW

I went on a Creative England training initiative, Market Trader, where they took a dozen producers to the Berlin Film Market. They helped us shape our pitches by making us write our film briefs on the back of postcards. You get great clarity from being able to sum up a project clearly in a few lines.

ANNE LAURILA: Whatever your film project or pitch, explain it in a few words. Imagine you are holding a glass of wine at a networking event at a major festival. You have two minutes or less to get the person you are talking to engaged, interested and understanding exactly what it is about. All that, surrounded by people and in a noisy environment. That, quickly, clearly and with enthusiasm. That is also how I explain the Finnish cash rebate system.

This is an example of a film I am currently developing with the support of Northern Ireland Screen.

Touched (feature)

Tara's baby won't survive birth. Devastated, she retreats to an island whose inhabitants are strange, their practices earthy. Then the baby's heart starts beating again.

Genre: psychological horror

Writer-director: Aislinn Clarke

Period: present day

Setting: UK/Ireland

Comps: *Rosemary's Baby, The Wicker Man, The Village*

Development funding: Northern Ireland Screen

Listing the genre tells people what to expect and listing comparable films gives a professional clarity. This gives any financier or interested party a clear understanding of the type of film you're going to shoot so you can draw them in to want to read the whole script – which will be the ultimate deciding factor.

ROCLIFFE NOTES on...
FILM PACKAGES

Have an outline of the entire film project and a script. Create a producer's statement about why you want to tell this story and how key budgetary or scheduling concerns will be tackled. A strong package prospectus is a good selling tool.

Sending out an advance email pitch is as simple as an email with a couple of lines about the project (25-word summary, genre, who is attached) and the invite to the receiver asking if they'd like to read the script. Depending on time of year if it is festival or award season it will take time for the person to respond.

It can complement the script and be a living document, which is augmented as you go along:

- One-line synopsis
- Bios of director, writer, producer

Depending how far along you are, include:

- List of HoDs, if any
- List of cast attached, if any – you will need LOIs (letters of interest)

Soft money (funding from national film bodies – Screen Ireland, British Film Institute – or subsidies); funders will want:

- Writer notes
- Producer notes
- Director notes

Sales companies and financiers may want:

- Finance plan
- Budget
- Shooting schedule

- Production schedule
- Lookbook or director's vision
- Sales estimates (most financiers will want to see these)
- Proof of ownership/rights
- Audience distribution/sales plan
- Recoupment plan (how the film is going to make its money back)

··

A DIRECTOR'S VISION

Jonathan Swift said 'Vision is the art of seeing things invisible'.

The biggest decision you'll make as a director is when you write how you're going to shoot the film and create this magical world. While you don't know what will be filmed, you have to have a strong concept of what it will be about (theme), how it will look and what it will feel like.

Newer directors are sometimes wary of sharing their vision of the film, in case people judge or question their creativity. That will happen anyway. The job of a director isn't simply to capture what people are saying on camera, shooting the dialogue – it's to reveal the world of the characters. Share and keep sharing and discuss.

Before a film is made there are many ways a director can prepare. They can create shot lists and storyboards of how they would ideally like the film to be. On the day of shooting, a director may throw away the shot list as the scene unfolds – it isn't that you have to stick rigidly to it; it's about communicating the idea and vision. Yes, much of this can come once they know the locations, and the cinematographer and production designer are on board, but there's no reason why you can't prepare these things in advance, and many funding rounds will expect to see them.

A director's statement is ever-changing; any time the script changes so will the document.

ROCLIFFE NOTES on…
DIRECTORS' STATEMENTS

- Open with a one-line synopsis – 25 words or so.

- Why do you want to tell this story?

- What was it that piqued your interest in this script/story?

- Subject/theme – what is the work about? Is there a moral behind it? What other themes are explored? Is there subtext?

- Structure/form – the sequence of events, the shape, rhythm, pace, feel.

- Visuals – the look/style.

- Sound – music, voice, script, atmosphere (including post sound, voiceover, silence).

- Technique – how the work will be realised and the methods you will use.

- Visual imagery – do you have anything in mind? Think *Schindler's List* and red dress, *Don't Look Now* and red coat.

- Support materials: storyboards, images of locations, casting wish list, filmic references.

- Inspiration: are there any existing movies, songs, works of art, or literary works you'd like to use as inspiration?

- Describe the type of person you'd want to cast in each role.

- Some directors use sizzle reels (clips of other movies sewn together) or storyboards.

THINGS LEARNT ON THE JOB

It's hard to know it at the time, but falling on your face is a rite of passage. Mistakes aren't bad for a producer – you fall but you become stronger, smarter, more learned and more confident. Just don't make yourself a prisoner of bad decisions or choices. Another biggie – don't be afraid to laugh on set; no one will take you any less seriously for laughing. The director and producer set the tone. Messing around is out but try to keep the atmosphere friendly. Come in every day and say hello to people and goodbye at the end of the day – it's professional and polite. Sometimes, after lunch, most crews can be a bit sluggish and need to warm up again. Stay away from the crafts table and the biscuits. Try to eat bananas, fruit and drink lots of water. Look after yourself. Be respectful of both crew and cast – neither is superior to the other.

ADO YOSHIZAKI: I never made a short film, much to my regret. I wish I had. I jumped straight from associate producer (which in reality covered a far greater proportion of production and business affairs than the title suggested) to full producer on my debut feature. Before being associate producer, I had probably clocked up around two or three years' experience in the production company's office, soaking up as much knowledge as possible. I had a decent understanding of most aspects of the business – financial, distribution and sales sides of things – but very little on-set and physical production experience. Post-production-wise, I had a decent understanding from my associate producer role and, overall (since the film was not always a happy experience), a good understanding of how I didn't want to produce a film! Everything was a big leap and it all came down to shouldering the full responsibility for every department of the film from development through to delivery. Suddenly, you find yourself in charge of the whole filmmaking machinery, and getting to delivery is a marathon with so many obstacles to overcome on the way. You have time, though, to learn and find your feet as you're completely absorbed in it and post-production is a good time to assess your journey and take a breather to gather strength for the finish line.

ANNA GRIFFIN: Get as much sleep as you can and never be afraid to ask for advice. Never blag it. If something's not clear, ask for clarity, whether you're dealing with financiers, a crew member, a health and safety advisor or a post-production company. Always make sure you've got things clear in your head because you're the one that's got to communicate to everyone else. You do not want to be in a position where something is going on around you and you're unclear as to why.

SEAN BAKER: I recommend that filmmakers know all aspects – a director should know the technical side of things as you may end up wearing other hats. I was the cinematographer on *Prince of Broadway* and *Take Out*. I don't like doing it but I had to because of the limited budget, and I couldn't ask people for that big a favour at that point in my career. When you are starting out, asking for favours is fine. You have to learn how to hustle. Not in an illegal way, but find ways to cut costs, look for discounts – embrace the limitations.

HELEN SIMMONS: From a producing point of view, the things I wish I'd been told before making my first feature are almost all related to erring a little more on the side of caution. You'll definitely need more contingency than you think (or hope). Things will definitely cost a little more in post (so up that budget before you shoot). You will most likely not get into Sundance. You'll probably have to think about an alternative distribution model to the traditional 'sales agent → distributor → loads of cinemas' one. You probably won't make any backend. But all of these things ultimately don't matter. Because at each step of the way you find the joy and success in the alternative. For me, it was going to some wonderful European festivals and having a brilliant time; learning how to self-distribute a film and make that a success; discovering that the real value in making the movie was the chance to be recognised as a producer and go on to make more films. But being more cautious would probably have saved a lot of time and effort, and having backup plans is essential. You haven't got into your festival of choice, so how many others are you waiting to hear back from? You haven't found a sales agent, so how are you going to get this film in cinemas as quickly as you can? Planning out every possible route is something I would recommend everyone do before they've even shot the movie. It's not being negative, it's being realistic, and when you do get into Sundance, it'll taste even sweeter.

RORY DUNGAN: There is NOTHING more important in filmmaking than the script. Everything stems from it. If you're not getting financed, it's often the script. Even if you convince yourself it's 'because it's a first-time director', which may well be part of it, it could easily be the script not being finance-ready. And even when you are financed, it doesn't mean the script is necessarily ready yet. Keep working, working and working some more at it. I recommend read throughs, shoot a dry run in a room with actor friends, cut together the DIY dry run, test it and probe it for weaknesses, then work on the script some more. Script development is the cheapest part of the entire process but it's 100% the best money you can ever spend on a film.

PETER SMYTH: I chose to save money in a couple of key areas that really caused headaches later on and it was making false economies. I had the best intentions at the time but if I were to go back and produce my first feature over again, I know I would be able to make a better film. The biggest leap was setting up a company and structuring it in such a way as to protect both the financier and the producers, complying with employment law, tax law, VAT, etc. It's all fairly straightforward but it's typically not something one encounters on short films. The difficulty with micro-budget features is that the producer has to do all this himself!

CAMILLE GATIN: Learning to delegate helped me keep my sanity and, more importantly, made for a better film. Don't do too much yourself. Trust your instincts. You always know whether someone is going to fit on the project or not when you meet them. Listen to that voice in your head and do something about it.

MANON ARDISSON: You have a lot less support because you can hire fewer people, and that means you as the producer have to take on board an insane amount of work. As I said, I think you (and your co-producer if you're lucky enough to have one) need to be a solo pre-prep production team to really think ahead and make savings in the long run in terms of crew, cast and locations. But you're not being paid for that time and you can't afford to pay anyone to support you. It's also difficult to manage the director's expectations, who of course has been waiting for so long to make that film and isn't willing to compromise, but doesn't necessarily understand the very real limitations on the production's resources. The fact that you will either be paid really little – or in some instances asked to defer your fee – means you need to find other ways to survive while working 24/7 on the film.

AISLINN CLARKE: When I set out to make *The Devil's Doorway* I had already directed quite a few large-scale theatre productions, and there are actually quite a lot of similarities between these two otherwise very different forms. For example, I'm very comfortable working with actors. I was also comfortable being at the helm of a production with a lot of moving parts and crew. Most of my surprises came later, with distribution, sales agents, and things like that. In theatre, once investment is made in a director, you're treated and trusted like an artist and left to your own devices. What you create is largely between you and the audience, via your cast and crew. It's quite different in film, where you have to answer to many people – funders, producers, executive producers, sales agents and distributors – before a single audience member sees your work. Film is much more cautious than theatre and that has been a learning curve for me.

SARAH BROCKLEHURST: Make sure your project is suited to a low budget (e.g. contained in just a few cheaply or freely available locations) and has a strong and distinctive voice and vision. Cast the best actors you can get, and give crew opportunities to step up (e.g. from camera operator to DoP) so that everyone is gaining something by being part of the film. It will be difficult and probably very messy, but there is merit to learning through your mistakes without the scrutiny and pressure of industry financiers, and aside from the practical and creative skills you will hone, your determination and tenacity will be tested, and those are qualities that will stand you in good stead for the rest of your career.

JONNY PATERSON: With post-production I learned not to micro-manage in as much as it is possible. You hire professionals to do a job and I find that people work best when you empower them to make decisions as opposed to trying to be in control of all those decisions. Of course, from a macro perspective it's important to be in control of the process, but on the micro level I found it important not to get too involved until I was asked for feedback. I'd advise this approach. Also, before I made my first short film, I had never worked on a physical set before, so that three-day shoot taught me so much. Actually, having made a feature film now as well, I can comfortably say that there isn't a huge difference between features and shorts when it comes to the physical production. The main variable is time and the number of days you have to get what you need, but the pressures and intensity are very similar on both.

FILMS THAT PUNCHED ABOVE THEIR BUDGETS

The low-budget model can work. *Lady Macbeth*, made for £500,000, worked brilliantly because they kept it simple – a main location, exterior shots, limited characters, superb costumes but not overly lavish. The performances are incredible and it managed to cross over. *Lady Macbeth* began its rollout in April 2017, and at the time of writing has grossed more than £800,000 in the UK and $3.2 million worldwide. Key territories where the film has been released so far are France ($986,000), Spain ($633,000), Netherlands ($310,000) and Italy ($129,000).

FODHLA CRONIN O'REILLY: We hired a castle, the location of which was recommended by Northern Film and Media. We were there for ten weeks: six weeks' prep and four weeks' shoot. It was like having a mini-studio for the entire time. It kept everyone together. It was about creating an atmosphere that was collaborative and creative. When people were happy working, they gave us their all. The first thing I had to do was secure a location, as this was the key thing. I booked it a year in advance. Once I had that and it was within budget the rest fell into place. We had accommodation at a local holiday village. I used all the contacts from commercials I had made in the past and they trusted me. I was transparent with the cast and crew about what our film was and what we were able to offer in terms of fees. We paid everyone on MFN rates at each level. I gave all shooting crew a small amount of backend [percentage of producer's net profit] and they felt like they owned what they were creating.

PAUL SNG: With *Dispossession* the film was made on a micro-budget of £35,000 that covered filming, editing and post-production, and £10,000 to cover marketing and distribution costs. The film has grossed over £73,000 in box-office receipts to date and was released by Verve on home entertainment in late October 2017. This was through very careful and sensitive marketing, given the film was released five days before Grenfell.

MANON ARDISSON: As of November 2017, *God's Own Country* had made over £800,000 at the UK box office. With regards to the production consideration, we shot on a working farm, which we found thanks to farmer Martin, who is a friend of the director Francis Lee's dad and helped us with the location scouting and animal handling. The other locations were found nearby so that our unit base was the same as the production office and we didn't have to pay for trailers, etc. We had five weeks' prep and six weeks' shoot, in story order. Like Fodhla, we were transparent with the cast and crew about the budget and everyone was paid MFN rates at each level.

FINANCING

The question is not how much do you need to make a film, but rather how much do you need to make things start to happen. This can work in a number of ways:

Budget for what you need to make the film and work towards raising that amount of money.

OR

You are given an amount of money (through a scheme such as Microwave/Catalyst/iFeatures) and you look at ways to make the film for that budget.

OR

You consult with a friendly sales consultant to understand how the marketplace would look at the film based on the elements in place. It could be that the film is very arthouse or that the budget is too high. They may look at the script and genre, and tell you where the project sits in the marketplace and what budget figure to put the film at. The sales estimates give you an idea of what sort of money the film can potentially make back – with no guarantees, of course.

EMILY MORGAN: Speaking with a sales agent is an important step. Keeping the budget realistic and having a clear idea of a film's ability to recoup is vital – unless you have cultural funding specifically for kick-starting new talent or showing important subject matters on-screen.

THE ROUTES TO INVESTMENT

Most films happen through sheer willpower. Not necessarily the most sensible approach but this is a non-exact science. No filmmaker's journey is the same and there is <u>no</u> singular route to financing. There aren't a huge amount of film-funding organisations providing subsidies for film so it's easy to research. You can't make a film entirely from subsidy or soft money. Usually you need at least 30% of real money in your budget, be it equity investment or the all-too-rare pre-sales.

EMILY MORGAN: Using soft-money option applications is a great way to focus a project. Every application, however successful, is helpful for moving the project forward.

TYPES OF FUNDING FOR INDIE FILMS

There are many ways to skin a cat. The majority of people start by crowdfunding their films, particularly shorts.

There are countless stories of people who struggled to get their first film financed. Christopher Nolan had no money so shot his first feature film, *Following*, over the course of a year. The Coen Brothers struggled to raise $750,000 for their first film *Blood Simple* in 1984 but got 65 private investors (doctors and small-business owners) to each contribute between $5,000 and $10,000, and the film grossed $4 million at the box office. Robert Rodriguez rented his body for medical tests to fund *El Mariachi*. On my first short, *No Deposit, No Return*, my fellow producers and I asked every man we met at the Cannes Film Festival to donate their sperm and give us the proceeds – and we pulled it off.

You will no doubt use a variety of different options to finance your film. A finance plan will outline how the film is going to be put together or packaged. It is unusual, although not altogether unknown, to have a single financier or source of revenue on a film – although this is more likely on schemes or with private equity.

This is a risk-taking business! When financing a film seek legal advice from a media lawyer and an accountant.

Soft money is funding from bodies such as Screen Ireland or the British Film Institute, or tax credits. Hard money is equity – think RTE, Film Four, BBC Films, Pathé, studios, private investors, gap financing and loans, post-production deals, deferred fees.

EMILY MORGAN: I believe it's better to work longer on your idea and package until you've raised enough money to actually make the film properly, unless it's money you're 100% sure you're not relying on arriving in the future. Whatever route you take, always seek legal advice.

RORY DUNGAN: If financiers need more convincing of your director's talents – make a short with that director. Set the short in the world of the film. Use it as a calling card if you fail to access finance from your national film fund, and get out to the market and meet sales agents and meet the American agencies that can financially package the film, with your short film and your script in hand. Between the sales agents and the agencies, like CAA, WME, UTA, etc., they'll know who might be interested in your project and you can finance through the market if someone is willing to take a chance on you. If not, or if you want to go down a different route, look at the soft funds throughout Europe and talk to potential co-producers about the project. Find out if they think it has a chance with their national funder. In a scenario where you can't get finance from your own national fund, and you need to entirely move the project elsewhere, it could be that the setting of the story or the characters or the language need to change. Then you have to make a judgement call on whether you're willing to do that, in order to get it made. Think outside the box and find other films similar to yours. Find out how they got made and where their finance came from. Pick up the phone, meet people, don't hide behind emails that are easily ignored. Be confident that you have a great script, because if you're not, then either it's too early, or you shouldn't be involved.

BROADCASTERS

Many television broadcasters and online platforms invest in films. They put in equity for the rights to screen the film.

- Amazon
- ARTE
- BBC FILMS
- FILM4
- Netflix
- RTE
- SKY

CROWDFUNDING

With *No Deposit, No Return*, we were one of the first to do a big crowdfunding campaign which hit all the newspapers. Through asking men to donate sperm we raised £60,000 in sponsorship, a lot of attention for the project and in-kind support as well as enough money to finance the elements of the shoot you have to pay for – catering, insurance, petrol and transport. It gave us a following and the marketing was amazing – we were given accolades such as best pitch in Cannes by a film journalist and were written about in the *Financial Times*, *The Times* and every industry paper. We hadn't even made the film and yet had amassed a credible following. Looking back, I regret we didn't just make a feature. At the time, financing films in this way was unusual, but in the last few years it has taken off.

For the feature *Nina Forever*, the producer and directors used crowdfunding for a particular scene. *My Name Is Emily* did a campaign to raise money for special equipment and support for Simon Fitzmaurice, who had MND (ALS). Zach Braff crowdfunded for *Wish I Was Here*, raising $3 million.

Crowdfunding is getting donations that don't need to be repaid, and there is no interest or premium on the money raised. Each of the platforms charges a different fee, but the filmmaker retains control of the film and keeps the profits. By tapping into the bank of love (family and friends) for small donations of £20, with 200 donors you can raise enough to make a short film.

Look at Indiegogo, Kickstarter, Seed&Spark.

CO-PRODUCTIONS

You can work with producers from other countries to access local funding abroad. To do this you need to engage with producers who have co-production agreements with your country. They will come on board and produce part of the film and bring funding with them. This may mean shooting or doing some post in that country; however, that isn't a bad thing, and this is a very effective way to increase your budget.

You may also attract them to your country and pick up your fee on their projects. You can meet co-production partners at film markets. Alternatively, contact a local film body for a list of local producers.

Before a festival market, reach out to film bodies to get contact details and meet with potential co-producers at markets like Cannes. There you can discuss potential co-productions able to avail themselves of local incentives and cash rebates. Markets and producer-training initiatives such as ACE and EAVE are great places to meet other producers.

> **ACE** – www.ace-producers.com
> **EAVE** – http://eave.org

UK Co-production Information
http://www.bfi.org.uk/supporting-uk-film/production-development-funding/international-co-production-funding

European Film Agency Directors
http://www.efads.eu/category/about

Cine-Regio – Some of the regional financiers in Europe
https://www.cineregio.org

European Audiovisual Observatory
www.obs.coe.int/en/national-overview

DEFERRED PAYMENTS

Many times I've been asked to 'defer my fees'. This means being paid later but only when the film is in profit. Most producers will at some point have deferred part or all of their fees. It isn't unusual for films made with low or micro-budgets to be financed in this way. You still need to have a proper budget, contracts that include this and are legally binding, and a collection account management agreement (CAMA) with a collection agency. You should really try to avoid deferment – it's not fair on producers to work continuously on films for free – but it does mean you have less money to raise.

The problem with fee deferment is that you don't get the money back unless the film is successful. So essentially that means not getting paid until after the film is in profit, and more often than not your position in the recoupment schedule is after investors and loans have been paid off.

EQUITY

This is by definition a term used to describe investors who contribute private finance to the film in return for a share or part-ownership of it, where their investment will be returned through the profits of the film. There are a million and one ways to structure the deal, but what needs to be clear is how the investor will see a profit, how the investor will recoup their investment and what ownership or 'rights' the investor gets in return for their investment. This needs to be legally and clearly defined. Be clear with whomever is financing you; films rarely make money back and you want to make sure your investor knows that and doesn't feel misrepresented. You must use a solicitor for any equity deals that outline the mutual funding agreement and recoupment plan.

LOANS

These are sums of money made available for the purpose of investment in the production costs of the film only. Sometimes the film is used as collateral. The warnings that go with this kind of loan should be adhered to, as the filmmaker is on the line for repayment of any unpaid amounts, so again seek legal advice.

GAP FINANCING OR FACILITY

Gap is a very expensive way to finance a film and has a high premium. It is generally used to fill the gap in the financing as money comes through. Sometimes you have people bankrolling the tax credit, but this usually comes with a premium or capitalised interest sum and is taken against a personal guarantee. Gap tends to be paid back first.

MUSIC

You can get deals from certain labels, but this relates only to the musical elements. Music elevates a film's production values. You can do an equity deal with a music label but this is rare.

PACKAGING BY AN AGENCY

Several of the major US agencies may come on board to build a film into a package by attaching talent they represent (writers, directors, actors, key crew) and securing finance for a fee, which is paid to the agency. They won't take just any project and are very discerning. It's tough to get them on board but very useful when you do.

The 'Big 6' are APA, CAA, ICM, Paradigm, UTA, WME.

POST-PRODUCTION EQUITY DEALS

A post-production company will give you their services as an investment in the film. As with any equity, this is priced at and in place of the normal fee. This gives them an equity stake in the film. There are many deals available and these can be favourable to the project and reduce costs. Their equity stake will tend to be at the normal rate of their work.

PRE-SALES

When you send a film to a sales agent they will expect you to present a script, a budget top sheet, any cast attached and the team. From this they will give sales estimates which determine the value of the film in various territories, by media, over time. With these sales you can borrow or finance against them. Distributors may buy in advance; sales agents may offer a minimum guarantee, which a bank or investor may loan against; financing co-producers may come on board. It is unusual to get pre-sales on films made for lower or micro-budgets with little or no star pulling power, although horror and religious films may fare better.

PRODUCT PLACEMENT

Product placement is thought to be a source of financing, but the brands are very unlikely to put their money into your film without a viable marketing strategy. What you can do is contact companies and get products, which can be used in the film pre-cleared (see clearance section). This can save on props and dressing. Some brands pay to be in films; however, the reality is that, unless you're a big brand movie like Bond, this is highly unlikely.

SOFT MONEY – FUNDING BODIES

Funding bodies from around the world invest in their own film businesses in order to develop and support original indigenous filmmakers and films, and to increase the audiences who can enjoy them. These are film grants, which will need to be repaid. In the UK and Ireland we are fortunate enough to have soft-money entities.

Soft-money sources are a great way to start. These routes are crowded and they can't fund everyone but the important thing is to keep trying. The first thing to do is get on their mailing lists and put any of their deadlines into your diary. Look up each region (you should also look overseas), as there are great schemes and incentives to be found. Here are a few:

- British Film Institute (BFI)
- Cine-Regio – Network of Regional Financiers in Europe
  www.cineregio.org/
- Creative England
- Creative Europe
- Creative Scotland

- European Audiovisual Observatory by country
  www.obs.coe.int/en/national-overview
- European Film Agency Directors
  www.efads.eu/category/about
- Ffilm Cymru Wales (formerly Film Agency Wales)
- Film London
- Northern Ireland Screen
- Screen Ireland (SI)
- Screen Yorkshire
- Wellcome Trust

TAX INCENTIVE/CASH REBATE

Tax incentives or cash rebates can be a really useful way of bringing in money for your film. Some incentives are more valuable than others. There are restrictions: there is usually a cap on the overall amount that can be claimed and you generally only claim on local expenditure in the country offering the tax credit or cash rebate. The tax credit does not have to be paid back, which is why it's so attractive and why each government pays close attention to it.

Read the guidelines carefully and, if you don't understand, ask the local film body. These change from year to year so you need to check the latest information.

For example, in the UK films must be for theatrical release and only certain elements in the budget qualify and an audit will be required. The film production company (FPC) responsible for the film needs to be within the UK corporation tax net.

UK TAX LINK:

www.gov.uk/hmrc-internal-manuals/film-production-company-manual

In Ireland, media lawyers and accountants can provide advice about Ireland's film and TV tax credit.

IRISH TAX LINK:

www.revenue.ie/en/companies-and-charities/documents/film-relief-application-form.pdf

ROCLIFFE NOTES on...

FILM FUNDING FACT FINDING

- Begin by looking at national film-funding bodies for the break-through and new talent schemes. Each country has different rules and regulations regarding funding and operates under a system that works for them. The web is your greatest ally.

- Go to film markets – AFM, Cannes, Berlin, Galway, Toronto, Rotterdam. Galway Film Fleadh is great for market first-timers as Cannes can be overwhelming – albeit a filmmaker's rite of passage. Book meetings with film bodies as soon as you book flights. Look at the list of Q&As and masterclasses. Check the delegates list.

- Read up on the tax-credit and tax-rebate systems. Note that the tax-credit and rebate situation changes every year depending on government changes or leadership of the organisation.

- Sign up for filmmaker training days with funding bodies and masterclasses and talk to other filmmakers. BAFTA run great masterclasses.

- Short-film funds tend to run on a rolling scheme. Check your local film office (borough and county) and ask about arts funding.

- Research SEIS and EIS schemes, i.e. private equity.

- TV broadcasters fund shorts and features – check their websites to see what funds they have available.

- Watch movies and read the credits to see who the executive producers and production company were. Then get in touch with those companies to ask for advice.

- Go to local film festivals and filmmaker-networking sessions – no one likes networking but consider this a fact-finding mission.

> **DEVELOPMENT LOANS**
>
> Most schemes have a development budget spreadsheet you can use.
>
> This funding is usually a loan and is paid in tranches.
>
> It must be repaid on the first day of principal photography.
>
> This generally doesn't cover full-on legals but includes an option agreement and is enough to get the ball rolling.

DEVELOPMENT FUNDING COVERS

- Option fees
- Scriptwriting fees
- Script editor
- Director expenses/low development fees
- Research
- Packaging
- Market & festival visits
- Casting to attach leads
- Research
- Budgeting
- Scheduling
- Legals
- Accounts
- Travel (recces/meetings)
- Producer expenses/low fees

PRODUCTION FUNDING COVERS

- Pre-production costs
- Shooting costs
- Post-production costs
- Marketing materials: poster, trailer, EPK, stills
- Deliverables – both technical and paperwork
- Festival attendance

CHAIN OF TITLE

Who owns the film? There can sometimes be several third-party agreements.

The documentation showing how each 'chain' can be traced back to the original owner of the work can include:

Adaptation rights

Copyright registration

Consent/life right

Development agreement

Option agreement

Producer agreement

Writer/director agreement

WHAT'S IN IT FOR AN INVESTOR?

Some investors want to expand their portfolio, or love films and see this as a way in. Whatever the reason, a form of return on investment and an idea of what they are investing in is expected.

Everything about financing a film begins with the rights. A writer may sell the rights to their script to a producer. To prove you have permission to make the film you need to show chain of title (option, attachment letter, purchase agreement). Once the producer owns the rights, they sell some of those rights, or an equity stake in the film, to raise the budget to make it. The rights are what get divided up and sold along the way.

A **competitive rate of return** may well be the reason someone backs your film and that may mean, although there is no guarantee of it, a financial profit. Offer an equity investor a higher percentage on their investment depending on their position and the amount they put in and this is what will be paid back. This can be 20%, e.g. if they invest £100 the return is £120. Pari passu (meaning the same rate/time) is where all investors are on an equal footing and paid back.

> **BACKEND OR PERCENTAGE OF NET PROFITS AKA PRODUCER NET PROFITS**
>
> A film has 100 percentage points.
>
> My experience of the breakdown has been 50% to investors and 50% to talent pool. Every project differs.
>
> The talent pool is made up of producers, director, cast and other key talent.
>
> Some no-to-low-budget films will offer a shared 1% to all HoDs and a shared 1% to crew.
>
> There are only ever 100 points on offer.

Another incentive is net profit – in other words offering a percentage of **backend** to investors or talent. This will only happen when the gross profits or those in first position have been paid off.

Some people invest because they want to get into films. To make their investment with you more attractive you can offer them a **credit** such as Executive Producer.

In the UK other incentives used include **tax relief** from the HMRC (for EIS/SEIS schemes). You can also offer investors visits to the set, red-carpet events and tickets to the celebrity premiere.

Film investment is precarious. What makes one film seem more risky than others? A first-time director, first-time producer, no-name actors, a very high budget, a challenging subject matter, and a specialised or niche audience – all these are deemed high risk. BUT, before you lose hope, none of this makes it impossible.

The truth is, films get made because people believe they are buying into a great script, creative vision and the commercial and entrepreneurial energy behind it.

Whatever you do, try not to suggest to someone that they're going to ride to success on your coat-tails. It's not a great way to start.

FINANCE PLAN

When I was first asked to create one of these I thought it would be a very complicated thing, but it sounds much more convoluted than it actually is. All a finance plan does is show where the money is going to come from and what is already there.

••

ROCLIFFE NOTES on…
FINANCE PLAN

- A finance plan, in its simplest form, is a document that outlines how you are going to finance your film.
- Clearly label the document as Finance Plan.
- List your cash budget.
- List any deferred fees.
- Total it.
- List who the different financiers are and what percentage of the budget they are contributing.

••

SAMPLE FINANCE PLAN

Finance Plan – Month Year – Film Title

TOTAL BUDGET 204,000

Source	Type	Return	%	Amount
Above the Line Deferral	Equity	Gross, Deferral and Net Participation	9.8%	20,000
Producer's Tax Credit	Rebate	Calculated at 25% of Qualifying Costs	16.7%	34,000
Private Equity	Equity	Gross, Deferral and Net Participation	73.5%	150,000
			100%	204,000

MEETING WITH A FINANCIER

Like any meeting, turning up and winging it with a potential financier isn't going to fly. You really need to know your script inside out. They are meeting you because of what's in it for them and the one thing you can do for yourself is know the story.

This is where a treatment comes in handy but, more than anything else, the thought process is essential. Don't overpromise and under-deliver. You don't know if the film will get into Cannes or not. You cannot guarantee an actor will be in it just because they went to school with you.

ADO YOSHIZAKI: Talk to investors and find out their motivations for investing and their needs. If the motivation is artistic or linked to attention and prestige, work on a festival strategy and take advantage of any prizes or nominations that could be forthcoming. If the motivation is financial, give them the numbers they need. Find out what they fear. How can you make them feel more comfortable about investing in your film? Think and act like it's business. Stay away from funny, flaky or too-good-to-be-true money. Try all the traditional (and safest) financiers first. Team up with other producers if you can work together to make more than the sum of your parts.

EMILY MORGAN: Don't just bombard a financier. Listen to what they have to say. The sooner a one-way pitch becomes a conversation, the better.

• •

ROCLIFFE NOTES on...
MEETING A FINANCIER

- Prepare your package.

- Don't promise a return on investment – you cannot guarantee this.

- Know how much your film is going to cost to make so you know how much you need to raise.

- Ask in advance who you are meeting with and look them up. Ask if they are expecting any documents from you.

- Make eye contact with the person you are meeting; smile and engage. Most of all, demonstrate why you are the only person who can tell this story this way.

- At the end of the meeting, thank them for their comments and ask what the next step for them is. If they don't offer an answer as to when they'll be in touch, by all means ask what their usual turnaround time is for decisions.

- End by saying you look forward to hearing from them.

- Drop them a follow-up line saying thank you for the meeting. Don't harass and chase.

PRODUCERS' TIPS ON INVESTORS

Don't go in expecting or feeling entitled to be financed. Financiers have an obligation to their investors. They won't be put off by your lack of experience and if you can show that you have done your preparation and have a good idea, they may even get behind you. They may also suggest you bring a more experienced filmmaker on board (for a fee) to deliver that film. That is not unusual and it would be foolish to let your pride get in the way here. Collaboration can be brilliant.

BENNETT MCGHEE: My personal experience is financiers are far more open and responsive than many new producers might think. Studios, independent financiers, UK institutions like BBC, Film4, BFI. They're very welcoming to new producers but of course be armed/prepped to talk about more than just the script. Casting ideas, director ideas, audience, market, comparable films (that have done well) are always good to have thought about when meeting them about a project.

ANNA GRIFFIN: Always make sure you are aware of their recent work. What have been their recent successes? What, perhaps, have been their recent flops? Go in like you know what they're about. This gives them confidence that not only have you done your research but you've contacted them for a good reason. Pitching a project should be easy and you should love it. If you're finding a project difficult to talk about, it's probably not the right time to be pitching it. You can only pitch a project to the right financier once, so timing is crucial.

CARISSA BUFFEL & KEVIN MATUSOW: Show the best financial coverage possible for that project. Whether we build the package from the ground up internally or it is given to us as a submission, we, like many others, make sure, first, that the story/script is something we feel strongly about (on many levels, be it subject matter, commercial viability, etc.), then we either build or look for the best essential elements that go to make the story as saleable and viable in the marketplace as it can be.

Producer NICK THURLOW has been involved in many films, including *Moonlight*. Here he shares his advice on what you need to demonstrate:

- Do you absolutely LOVE the script, i.e. will you really pull for it when times get tough? Because they will.

- Is there cast attached? Who? This is the new critical for returning investor money.

- Do you KNOW the audience for the project?

- What is the single, one-line pitch? If you need a page to explain your script or project it's too complicated.

- How experienced is the director, as this may cause difficulty getting cast.

- How old is the package? If a project has done the rounds and still not found backing this often indicates a problem.

- Chain of title – how simple is it?

- Is the financing simple? Low-budget movies need to/should be kept straightforward. Not a hard and fast rule but an indicator of success is a simple finance plan.

- Avoid projects with more than four producers – too many cooks. Sometimes this can't be avoided but it becomes difficult to know who's doing what when there are too many people involved.

- Don't rely on others' opinion about what kind of soft money your project may be eligible for. Do all your own research on grants and tax credits. Keep in mind that laws and funding schemes can change quickly, so it's up to you to be up-to-date.

COMPLETION BOND

At the low- or micro-budget stage it is unlikely you will have a bond; however, it isn't unknown for financiers or investors to insist on one. It very much depends on the financier. Completion bonds aren't something to be scared of. These are professionals who will expect all the paperwork to be in order, but if anything goes wrong they'll have seen it before and be able to advise on how to proceed.

A completion bond is a written contract that guarantees a film will be finished and delivered on schedule and within budget. A producer usually secures one for the benefit of the bank or other financiers, who agree to make the necessary production funding strike price available to the producer. They oversee and support a production. The bond company will endeavour to minimise production risks through due diligence prior to the start of a production, and monitoring during it, until delivery of agreed final materials.

CLOSING FINANCING

This can be an absolute nightmare, with multiple copies of the paperwork legals in hand. Some financiers require an ink signature too.

A **transaction summary sheet** is a clear document that outlines all the terms of the film and is a very useful checklist.

Although you may not need some of them, it's quite normal to see on the list:

- Budget

> **TRANSACTION SUMMARY SHEET**
>
> A document that lists all the parties involved. It's an excellent template and checklist for closing. It covers recoupment, investors, budget, credits, etc.
>
> www.bfi.org.uk/sites/bfi.org.uk/files/downloads/bfi-transaction-summary-sheet-generic-template.pdf

- Collection Agency Management Agreement (CAMA) – they collect the funds a film makes from the distributor
- Cash-flow schedule
- (For UK) Pre-certificate needed for tax credit – apply via the BFI website – DCMS
- Complete financing package identifying all sources of finance and their recoupment position (finance plan and recoupment schedule)
- Completion bond
- Details of box office, award bonuses agreements
- Director contract
- Distribution report including sales estimates and pre-sales commitment by distributor and territory.
- Estimated value of any tax credits approved by an auditing company
- Finance and investor agreement
- Interparty agreement (ensures all financiers make their money available at the same time and sets out the contractual obligations and rights of all parties and the recoupment schedule)
- Letters from other committed financiers, including estimated cost of funds (when appropriate)
- Letters of intent from director and key cast/crew
- Producer's contract
- Production and post-production schedules
- Screenplay

- Shoot locations
- Transaction summary sheet
- Underlying works (if any)
- Writer contract
- Option agreement

CHALLENGES AND ADVANTAGES OF LOW-BUDGET FILMMAKING

Each project has its own unique requirements, and these will give you a first-hand insight into the things that work at lower-budget levels. A film made for a low or micro-budget means you're forced to think about solutions creatively, even more creatively than if you had the biggest budget in Hollywood – that's the key to low-budget filmmaking. Your job is to demonstrate that you can deliver the best version of your project and deliver it on budget. It can be done.

SEAN BAKER: The advantages of making a low-budget film are you can retain control of the movie if you are behind the money. More money is good to have because it means extra resources and time and extra equipment, but low-budget films make you creative because you can't throw money at the problems. You have to throw creativity at them instead. Think your way out of obstacles. It can lead to a wonderfully creative process and many happy accidents and serendipity. It makes you focus on character, dialogue and realistic portrayals of people – ultimately the things audiences connect with. You have to rely on really good storytelling not stunts and set pieces. The downside is that you have a lack of resources and time, and you don't make much money, and it's difficult to sustain a career like that and pay the bills at the same time. That said, it can work when you come up with a system like the filmmaker Jason Blum, who makes low-budget films and a tremendous profit from them.

SARAH BROCKLEHURST: One of the hard truths when setting out to make your first film is that no one owes you this opportunity. Until you've proven your talent, it's unlikely that conventional funding routes will support you, but if you feel ready you shouldn't wait for permission. You have to be inventive and resourceful when it comes to raising money: friends and family, crowdfunding, grants, sponsorship... all best approached with a clear, stylish and professional investment pack, so take pride in the way you present your project.

ADO YOSHIZAKI: We raised the money through a combination of getting pre-sales through Pathé, equity from the BFI and a post-deal with Pinewood (including stages and rooms), some gap and some Japanese equity that took a unique recoupment position that didn't negatively affect the others. The biggest challenge was time, time, time! We had a first-time director and, more than likely, in every such case, they take some time to adjust to the (quite) brutal scheduling. We fell quite far behind on day two and had the completion bond step in. Playing catch-up through the rest of the shoot meant hard decisions on what to keep and what to lose. Other than time, the biggest challenge was to not get overwhelmed by the amount of firefighting needed. It comes at you from all angles, and having to approach your financiers for more money during post-production is always quite unwelcome (but nearly always necessary!).

CAMILLE GATIN: Closing financing alone was the biggest challenge. It always comes across as this incomprehensible, uncontrollable alchemy between various financiers, but in the end there'll be lawyers to guide you through and your role is to strike the right balance with financiers between creative excitement for the project and a sense that everything is under control production-wise. It's always about who blinks first. Get that first financier and the others will follow. Ours was the BFI.

IAN BONHÔTE: As both a director and a producer and company owner, I have been feeling responsible for everything from day one. This is one of the biggest challenges on features. It might not be your fault if something goes wrong but it is your responsibility because you are in CHARGE! We raised almost all the money ourselves so we felt super responsible for every aspect of the film.

RORY DUNGAN: We wasted a year and a half on a project we'd set up with an American financier because we were so taken with getting the whole thing fully financed at a very generous budget level. We thought we'd made it! It took a year and a half to realise it wasn't going to work out and that we were pulling in different directions. It set the film, and realistically our careers, back by a year and a half. Because we had started making shorts with Screen Ireland and our feature films were also developed through funding with them, they have now been a major production financier on our first two feature films. We've also raised market money for one of these films through a sales agent we pitched to in Cannes and are co-producing with two different territories and accessing national funding in those territories. And one of the other projects I'm developing is on some market radars and will be a bigger budget again.

CHRISTINE HARTLAND: The feature-film-financing process is unique and recoupment was, and still can be, a learning curve, especially as budgets get higher. We were lucky that *WMD* and *Containment* both had one investor each and so that process was fairly straightforward. On *WMD*, some of the challenges were on a technical level as we were shooting with CCTV/surveillance cameras strapped to the bodies of video cameras and needed to make sure it would work on a big screen, which it did; and on the production side, filming abroad (Berlin, Rome and Washington) while trying to keep the same core crew over the 20-day shoot, spread from the end of January to early March due to cast availability, and all that on a micro-budget.

SARAH GAVRON: Making a low-budget feature is liberating in many ways as the pressure is less, so you have more freedom to make the film in the way you want. But filmmakers always need more shooting time and time is usually money. It's best to make films that fit the budget, so if low-budget, avoid period dramas with lots of effects and crowd scenes, etc.

MANON ARDISSON: I knew it was challenging to finance a film, but an LGBT drama from a first-time director is particularly tricky in terms of generating commercial interest. We had the opportunity to develop the film through iFeatures and that was a big turning point as public financiers became aware of the project. The BFI and Creative England understood the material much better, and financed the film the following year, outside of the iFeatures programme, but having become aware of the project thanks to it. I learnt about post-deals and financial closing the hard way – by doing it – but that was a good experience.

PETER SMYTH: The money was raised via a private equity financier who had just set up in media financing and production. It was the first film he had invested money in. His background was as a businessman and entrepreneur and his experience in these fields was very useful to the film. Our film is set primarily in a couple of council flats. It really should have been a studio build and studio shoot but our budget didn't quite stretch to that so we had to shoot in a real block of council flats in Southampton. The block was fully occupied by residents so it was a crazy thing to do really – the entire four-week shoot was there. But Southampton Council were so helpful and accommodating it made what should have been impossible just about doable. Also, the security issues and agreement with the council meant I had to live on set for four weeks, which really was a challenge.

DOMINIC BUCHANAN: You have to treat it like being a detective; it's homing in on leads, but also, and more importantly, it's about research and informed conversations with sales agents and distributors. If you're trying to raise money via high-net-worth individuals, you have to realise people with money don't necessarily want to be known, so it's finding the way in via various links. That being said, money can be raised within the industry – there's actually more money than ever before, just a lack of suitable projects for investors. The biggest challenge on my first feature was the lack of time combined with the lack of money.

JONNY PATERSON: For *Halfway*, my feature film, I raised all the money through private equity. I drew up a business plan that broke down the number I was looking to raise into 20 units and sold off those units either in singles or multiples. That is to say, I didn't know any one investor who could give me the whole lot, but I felt I might know 20 individuals who could each give me one twentieth of what I needed – or something along those lines.

SCHEDULING

Time is money and this is never more true than in the film business. Budgets and schedules are about the time it takes to make a film, which informs the cost.

Hiring kit and personnel is costly when working on films with low or micro-budgets as every penny counts, but many suppliers are happy to do a deal to support newer talent, although rarely for free.

GET STARTED

Let's assume you've raised some money. **<u>Set a date</u>**. This can be determined by an actor's availability, location availability or time of year. It should be far enough in the future not to terrify you and near enough that the money you've raised won't have lost its value.

<u>Start to plan</u> and keep planning. Be paranoid – question everything to see if it's been done.

Don't surprise people. Keep your cast and crew happy by agreeing all terms in advance. To move things along, you need to know how much money is required to get things started and how much time it will take – that's the reality of low-budget filmmaking.

A good place to start is by understanding the three sides of the triangle of business: **you can <u>only</u> pick two!**

You can get it done quickly and achieve high quality, but this will be costly.

You can do it quickly and cheaply, but it may not be good.

You can make it good and at low cost, but this will take time.

HOW LONG WILL TELL YOU HOW MUCH

There are several discussions you need to have before you commence scheduling. With low-budget filmmaking you often shoehorn the film into the number of days or weeks you can afford to shoot.

Break down a script by scheduling what's needed. A line producer usually does this for budgeting purposes. If you can't afford a line producer to do the initial budget, understand that it's a professional skill, but not a role you can't fill yourself. And this is unit call to unit call.

The shooting schedule will be redone by a 1st assistant director to reflect many factors, including the shot list and availability of actors and locations. A shooting schedule can be extremely tight due to a number of fast-moving parts – an extremely short prep, a limited number of days' principal photography, possibly six-day weeks.

The individual needs of each department should be met in order for them to be ready for camera. If they don't have the people-power, turnover on camera may be delayed and shoot time will be shortened.

As filmmakers, we have a duty of care to all personnel in all departments to diligently observe the minimum rest periods and turnaround provisions as they apply to the work schedules. **Safety is no accident** – I will say this a lot.

For some, this means staggering staffing throughout each shoot week in order to provide sufficient rest periods while taking full advantage of non-shooting business days for prep work. For others, it might mean relieving off-set crew from prepping locations or sets beyond their shoot week.

A SHOOTING WEEK

5-DAY WEEK – work 5 days straight with 2 days off.

6-DAY WEEK – work 6 days straight with 2 days off.

11-DAY FORTNIGHT – work 6 days with one day off and then 5 days with 2 days off.

TURNAROUND – need 11 hours between wrap and call.

A SHOOTING DAY

12-HOUR DAY – this is 11 hours with 1 hour for lunch

11-HOUR DAY – this is 10 hours with 1 hour for lunch

CONTINUOUS DAY – you work through lunch and are compensated for the hour so crew are wrapped 2 hours earlier. On 12-hour days crew are wrapped after 10 hours and on 11-hour days crew are wrapped after 9 hours

SPLITS – working from after 10 am through the day into the evening, i.e. 11 am until 11 pm

NIGHTS – working through the night; you need to give a rest day at the end of the row of nights

You can claw back 1 hour a day. And this is unit call to unit call.

NOTE: Working hours and laws differ from country to country. Union rules differ so the above may not apply.

You need to be clear with crew that overtime isn't automatically paid if they work beyond the work week without this being agreed and approved first and in the budget.

Continuous days mean everyone gets home earlier and are savers when there is restricted access to a location or light dependence in winter. That said, they can be a strain on the make-up, assistant director and costume departments, and cast need to be on board. Catering also needs to be modified accordingly to food the crew can eat on the go.

Don't piss off your crew – don't break lunch break (which should happen five or five and a half hours after unit call) or turnaround.

ROCLIFFE NOTES on...

CREATING A SCHEDULE

- 1 page is calculated as 1 min and calculated in eighths.

- Always know that, however long you have to shoot, you'll wish you had more time.

- Cut the script before you start. Be clear about the scenes you don't need. Don't shoot them. Identify which parts of the script are luxuries that will end up on the cutting-room floor.

- Be aware of the legal obligations and different working-time rules for different countries as well as union rules.

- What style does the director want? Handheld, Steadicam, and do they want tracks? Tracks and Steadicam will take up more of the day. Handheld/static is quicker to shoot.

- The director and DoP need to tell you how they want to shoot. This isn't a shot list, but you need to schedule and they need to understand any restrictions.

- The best way to help a director and DoP understand the restrictions is to show them a schedule.

- How are you going to shoot each scene? This is decided by the amount of action, unit moves, special effects and crowd scenes. Talky two-handers are quicker to shoot, although you need a variety of shots to make them interesting.

- Do they want to shoot it in any particular order for any particular reason?

- What are the locations where travel time needs to be factored in? Every time you change location you lose at least an hour!

- Be prepared to change things as you go along – weather changes, a location falls through, etc.

- Health and safety is always a consideration; don't cut corners in terms of time or anything else that might compromise this.

- How many days can you afford to shoot?

- How many pages can you realistically shoot in a day? Don't wing it and hope for the best – or try and see what happens.

....

HOW MANY DAYS ARE NEEDED TO SHOOT?

We have a 4- or 5/6-day shoot – and that's a lot! How do you know? If you have 10 pages and 2 days to shoot them, that's 5 pages a day.

Try these out with a 90-page script:

Example 1

90 pages @ 4 pages per day = 22.5-day shoot
Can you afford 22.5 days? No, you can only afford 22 days.

Budget impact at a glance:

Crew at 22 days
Equipment for 4 weeks
Catering for 22 days

Recommend: 2 x 11-day fortnight – give everyone 2 days off to recover mid shoot. This way, if you fall behind, you have the possibility of a sixth day in week 4. Look at the script and see where you can cut 2 pages or whether you need to shoot more on certain days.

Example 2

90 pages @ 6 pages per day = 15 days to shoot

Budget impact at a glance:

Crew at 15 days
Equipment for 3 weeks
Catering for 15 days

Play around with different pages per day.

Recommend: 2 x 6-day weeks and 1 x 5-day week – give everyone 2 days off to recover mid shoot. This way, you reduce the page count to 5.5 and give yourself 17 days to shoot.

How to work out how much time it will take to shoot pages and make your daily page count:

If your daily page count is 5.5 pages a day and you're working a 10-hour day, divide 10 hours by 5.5 pages = 1 hour 49 mins per page.

NOTE: Convert the hours to minutes 10 x 60 = 600 ÷ 5.5 = 109 minutes per page.

Then you need to break down each scene into shots and time how long each shot will take. On shoots, a take refers to each filmed version of a particular shot or setup.

SCENARIO: A scene with two people talking is 1 4/8 pages.

Multiply 109 minutes by 1.5 = 163.5 mins (2 hours 43 mins). So you have 163.5 mins to complete the scene.

You have decided you want the following shots:

- Medium long shot wide running the entire scene so you have your master
- Single mid shot on each of the actors

- Extreme close-up on each of the actors
- Cutaways, coverage reaction shots

You're going to need a minimum of 2 takes on each.

SHOOTING RATIO:

This is often hard to understand: it is the duration of the footage shot in relation to what ends up on-screen. If you have 1 page of script which is equal to 1 minute and you shoot it 6 times – you have 6 minutes of footage. That means the shooting ratio is 6:1.

Average for first-timers is 15:1.

The higher the ratio, the more time you'll need in edit.

This means if your script is 90 pages, i.e. 90 mins, you will have 90 mins x 15 footage = 1,350 minutes.

This is 22 hours of footage to watch and cut down to 90 mins.

SETUP 1:

07.00 am – call time was 7 am.

40 mins spent setting up. Director rehearsal, actors are in hair, make-up, costume and travelling to set.

During this time, lighting and camera positions are agreed.

07.45 am – camera turnover.

Medium long shot – 90–100 seconds each x 3 takes = 5 minutes.

Lighting adjustments, make-up and costume checks, props reset between takes – allow 15 mins.

08.00 am – finished setup 1.

SETUP 2:

20 minutes spent changing camera lens and placing camera in new position. Some lighting adjustments. Mic adjustment on actor.

08.20 am – camera turnover.

Medium shot of Actor 1 speaking x 2 takes = 90 seconds x 2 takes = 3 minutes.

Lighting adjustments, make-up and costume checks, props reset between takes – allow 7 mins.

08.30 am – finished setup 2.

SETUP 3:

10 mins spent changing camera lens and position. Lighting adjustments.

08.40 am – camera turnover.

Close shot of Actor 1 face speaking x 2 takes = 90 seconds x 2 takes = 3 minutes.

Lighting adjustments, make-up and costume checks, props reset between takes – allow 7 mins.

08.50 am – finished setup 3.

SETUP 4:

20 minutes spent changing camera lens and position. Lighting adjustments. Mic adjustment on actor.

09.10 am – camera turnover.

Medium shot of Actor 2 speaking x 2 takes = 90 seconds x 2 takes = 3 minutes.

Lighting adjustments, make-up and costume checks, props reset between takes – allow 7 mins.

09.20 am – finished setup 4.

SETUP 5:

10 mins as DoP on camera and angle.

09.30 am – camera turnover.

Close shot of Actor 1 face speaking x 1 take = 90 seconds x 2 takes = 3 minutes.

Lighting adjustments, make-up and costume checks, props reset between takes – allow 7 mins.

09.40 am – finished setup 5.

SETUP 6:
DoP allow 10 mins to lift release camera from locked angle.

09.45 am – camera turnover.

DoP moves the camera around the room getting cutaways, close-ups on actors' hands and feet.

09.55 am – completed the scene.

LOOK AT THE CLOCK:

- 3 hours gone
- 7 shooting hours left
- 25 minutes behind schedule

You've made up for the time you lost setting up but you're still behind.

Lunch is in two hours and you still have 4 pages to go.

What do you do? Look at the shot list. Is there a shot you can drop or amalgamate?

Every day has to be planned out – with or without a 1st AD. You can see where you are and what you need to do to make the day. If you don't do this, you may have to drop a scene, or worse, not have enough footage to make a film.

••

ROCLIFFE NOTES on...
SCHEDULING

- Read the script ALL THE WAY THROUGH!
- Number all script scenes for scheduling.
- Use breakdown sheets or software like MM Scheduling, or use an Excel spreadsheet.

- Decide on a proposed start date for shooting.
- Have an idea of the style of shooting.
- What will the shooting ratio be?
- How long is the shoot?
- How many days in a shooting week?
- How many pages per day?
- Length of the shooting day (10–12 hours).
- 11- or 12-hour turnaround between days.
- Each script page equals one minute of screen time – doesn't matter how quickly/slowly it runs in your head.
- Remember the 1/8 rule can be misleading.
- Break down scenes into 1/8 of a page. Fold page in half, fold again and fold again, now you have it.
- Watch carefully for unscripted subscenes/implied shots.
- Watch out for changing character names/set names.
- Schedule scenes in one set together. Try not to return to a location later in the schedule. Try to put several sets in locations near each other to reduce unit moves.
- Look at which locations will have restrictions – for example, a busy street or station. It's often better to schedule exterior scenes early in the schedule with weather cover.
- Have weather-cover ideas as a backup plan for when things go wrong.
- See the ratio of day and night shooting – try to do all night shoots in one sequence, as you will require a rest day for the crew. If shooting at night you can split days, i.e. start at midday or later, and each day claw back an hour, i.e. call time at 3 pm, wrap at 2 am, then the next day you can call people an hour earlier at 2 pm, wrap at 1 am, and each day get the hour back.
- When shooting on water or near a beach, check the tide times.
- Anything involving water takes up to three times as long to shoot.

- When shooting in a particular season, how does that affect the shoot? Is it cold, is it rainy, are you shooting spring/summer in winter (leaves on trees)?

- Know the times of sunrise and sunset, for the amount of light or dark you will have.

- Artist availability – does a particular cast member's lack of availability impact the shoot and which scenes are shot when? Try to avoid one day a week for the three weeks.

- Animals will never do what you expect them to. There are specific guidelines and hours an animal can work. Consult an animal wrangler to factor in the hours.

- Children have restricted hours, i.e. difficult to do a night shoot, breaks and hours are all specified. Check regulations with PACT. Apply for a child licence minimum 4 weeks in advance. And provide professional chaperones.

- Stunts and special effects are timely, as you have to set up, rehearse and prep. Stunts are dangerous and you need to work with a qualified stunt coordinator. Don't think you can get away without one. Allow enough time to rehearse. The more complex the action or stunt, the more time will be needed, and something that may be 30 seconds of screen time may take a whole day to shoot.

- Never leave a stunt till the end of the day. Shoot the stunt action in order. This applies to music and dancing too, when you also need to have playback (some way of playing the music).

- Travelling shots and driving scenes are time-consuming to set up. Make the best of the time you have in a car. If you have a scene that involves driving along a road chatting, you'll use an A frame or low loader. If you need to close a road you have to have a police escort. You need to get permission before shooting on a motorway.

- Using big equipment like cranes is expensive and these take quite a while to set up. You should try to set up as much of your expensive equipment as possible in one day.

- Allow time for setting up lighting, set dressing and also striking time. This will eat into shoot time. You can ask electricians to do a pre-call but this could incur overtime, which is costly.

- Visual effects will take time to set up and get going and you'll be surprised where they occur.

DIFFERENT TYPES OF SCHEDULES

ONE-LINE/STRIP SCHEDULE

This is a short version of the shooting schedule and has basic information about it.

EXPANDED/SHOOTING SCHEDULE

This is a detailed outline of each day's shooting.

DAY OUT OF DAYS/CAST-ANIMALS-STUNTS-ARMOURERS

Lists which actors are working on which days and how many days they are required.

SWF | SW = Starts Work | Work = Working | WF/F = Finishes Work | SWF = is a daily and starts and finishes on that day.

▶ See Appendix for examples

ROCLIFFE NOTES on...

WORKING WITH SMALL CREWS

The fewer people you have, the more time you need to prep and shoot the day. The day starts at unit call and setup is part of the working day.

- You can never have enough meetings with Heads of Department. Start with a scene by scene where you talk through each scene. It will take a day to do.

- The art department needs time to set up, put the props in place, make sure the set is shoot ready, and then to strike the set (take it all away).

- Have tone meetings where DoP, production designer, costume designer, hair and make-up designer get together with director and producer and talk through the style, feel and tone of the production.

- The lighting department needs time to set up.

- The make-up department needs a minimum of 15–30 minutes per cast member and that's for simple make-up.

- The costume department needs time to get people changed.

- Rehearsing and blocking with actors on set means the art and lighting departments can't set up.

- Continuity is essential for tracking shots but they also spot things that would be costly to fix later in the edit or post.

- There are fewer people to do things.

- Having people helping out who have never experienced being on set isn't actually as useful as it sounds – they don't know what they're doing.

BUDGETING

Every budget and breakdown is unique to each project. There are budget templates but you need to get quotes and fill in the figures. Each script has its own price list, depending on its budget range, and can read like a shopping list. Sometimes you're given a clear idea of what that is and other times you have to see what it will cost.

To budget a script means listing every location, cast member, special prop, outdoor scene, nighttime scene, etc. Big props like cars (action vehicles), stunts and special effects are expensive (of course you haven't got these if you followed my notes on writing a film on a low or micro-budget). To avoid going over or under budget invest in a good accountant or someone who has bookkeeping experience and can add things up quickly and can monitor the spend.

A good production manager or line producer will have contacts they can call on to make the budget stretch to accommodate the scale of the project effectively.

TIME + MONEY + TALENT

There are three things to consider – time + money + talent – and you won't necessarily have the luxury of all three.

You need to start by realising there are three types of things on a film:

- The things that are necessities/essential
- The things you need
- The things that are a luxury

To start, create a **production schedule** to see the film from start to finish, including prep and wrap time for everyone. This may change as the production evolves.

Locations and logistics – shooting on location away from the city will cost money in travel but just outside the centre will be cheaper.

Don't leave any cost out. There is nothing worse than finding out you haven't put in a line for something you'll need later on. It's very difficult to find the money for it after the fact.

Is it worth being VAT registered? Discuss with your accountant.

APPROXIMATIONS FOR BUDGETING

These are for guide purposes only and change:

- Director, writer, producer fees are 1–3% of the budget – these are the first items to be reduced and go back into the budget or be deferred
- 1% insurance
- 5–10% contingency
- Check fringes (National Insurance, Pension, PAYE costs)
- The art department should be between 8% and 10% of the total budget, including crew and purchases
- Post-production might fall between 10% and 20% of the budget
- Catering estimate – between £8 and £15 per day per head
- Working hours will impact your budget
- Make sure you look at minimum rates of pay and living wages

THINGS TO GET QUOTES ON

Phone several suppliers and get the weekly cost (cheaper than daily) of equipment packages. Don't be afraid to haggle the costs down from first quotes. Also ask what the delivery and collection charges are and damages/replacement costs. You get better deals if you budget ahead of production, not during.

- Accounting packages
- Payroll services
- Camera
- Catering
- Lighting
- Grip
- Insurance cover
- Stunts
- Special effects
- Armourers
- Walkie-talkies
- Opening and closing titles
- Post-production quotes-- what is it going to cost you for a basic sound mix, grade?
- Car/van hire, and ask about 'excess insurance' as people are tired on shoots

THINGS TO CONSIDER INCLUDING IN A BUDGET

Things you may not have factored in, but which you should make an allowance for in case they come back to bite you, are:

- Graphics for artwork, book covers, newspapers
- Blacking out of windows
- The dreaded loss and damages!

STOCK FOOTAGE

iStock
Pond5
Shutterstock

- Put in an allowance for read throughs/rehearsals/fittings spaces
- Children need chaperones who will be paid
- Storage for props, costumes and kit
- Filming outside – if it's cold you may need thermals
- Skips and rubbish removal
- Electricity
- Deliverables – post items
- Stock/Archive footage and photos
- Street parking/car parks do a deal
- First-aid kits, fire extinguishers and fluorescent jackets
- Fuel is better than mileage as you can get VAT receipts and claim back the cost if you have registered for VAT
- Water can add up – so get a water cooler and supply everyone with water flasks at the beginning of the shoot (and write names on them)
- Bank charges
- Consumables – batteries, tape and markers
- Travel costs

ROCLIFFE NOTES on...
HOW TO BUDGET

My personal issue is **people saying to me we can get things for free**. I work on the assumption that nothing is for free but things can be blagged. You can rely on the kindness of strangers more than you can on your friends. Friends will cancel and let you down when it comes to the scene where you need loads of extras.

- Break the budget down into cast, crew, camera, sound, lighting, action vehicles, animals, stunts, art department, costume, make-up – and don't forget the locations.

- What have you spent in development already? Do you need to repay a development loan?

- Decide who is going on the recce days – you need to pay them. Be clear about prep.

- Have you budgeted for five- or six-day weeks? This needs to be in the contract.

- Don't pay below the national minimum wage (NMW).

- Get your HoDs to be realistic about who they need.

- The DoP often goes to the grade – is this time covered in their fee?

- The editor can start on the second day of the shoot.

- Doubles may be needed for stunts.

- If locations are in one place, consider Airbnb and put make-up, hair, costume, actors and unit base there.

- The higher the resolution (4K and above), the more hard drives you'll need.

- If you're using PACT/Equity contracts for actors you'll need to budget for the levy. The same is true for Skillset trainees.

- America actors on SAG will be on PACT/Equity global rule one deals which means you pay their pensions, health and welfare contributions.

PAYING PEOPLE AND EXPENSES

You can persuade people to work for free for a short period of time but always make sure they're not left out of pocket. Feed people well – breakfast and lunch – or give everyone a set lunch allowance, and keep the crew hydrated.

When paying people low wages, expect to swap them in and out if you're talking about longer than a few days. Experienced crew will work for low rates but may leave you in the lurch if a paid job comes along. This isn't personal; they just have to keep a roof over their heads.

- Everyone is paid expenses from runners to the DoP – pre-agree in writing and reimburse any travel costs such as train/tube/bus fares.

- Everyone is paid minimum wage, at an hourly rate plus holiday pay.

- Paying a low but decent rate with each level having parity – i.e. all HoDs are paid the same, the next level down are paid the same – means you'll be able to secure experienced people for longer.

- Check if people are PAYE or loan-out companies.

- Set down the ground rules – nothing is reimbursed unless it has been pre-agreed.

> To work out the weekly minimums take the national minimum wage hourly rate x shooting hours (10 or 11) x shoot days in the week.

ABOVE-THE-LINE COSTS

Above-the-line is a term that refers to the list of individuals who guide, influence and hopefully add to the creative direction, process and voice of a given narrative in a film and their related expenditures:

- Script/development – on shorts unlikely to have a fee

- Features may have a nominal fee, no more than 1%

- Fees for writer, director, producer

- Script editor – the great thing about many initiatives is you get script-editor feedback

- Pre-existing development costs or a loan that needs to be repaid?

- Producer/director fee – on shorts unlikely to have a fee, but features may have a nominal fee

- Executive producers

- Producers

- Co-producers
- Artists and casting director
- Expenses on a short – even a gesture goes down well
- PACT/Equity minimum rates for low and micro-budget features
- Costs for rehearsal/ADR/fittings
- Be clear about what special contractual requirements there are in the casting advice notice (CAN) – such as travel, hotels, etc.

> **CAN:**
> Casting Advice Notice – sets out the terms of ground transportation (to/from home). If you have to pay, request non-exclusive, ADR sessions, rehearsal, shoot period, etc. and special requirements, credits. Casting director will draw up and production will send out.

BELOW-THE-LINE COSTS

Below-the-line is a term referring to the individuals who work on the physical production of a given film, the post-production work, and all the related expenditures.

These costs cover positions which include, but are not limited to, the following:

- Key crew
- Non-starring cast
- Art department
- Costumes
- Locations
- Travel
- Catering

- Insurance
- Festivals – entry and attending

Below-the-line expenditures commonly fluctuate during production, which is why it's so important to include a CONTINGENCY!

- Holiday pay included
- National Insurance
- Allow time for prepping each set and clearing it
- Dailies – sparks, props, make-up, riggers, Steadicam
- Staffing levels for each department – be realistic
- Trainees – need to be paid unless they are in full-time education
- Have you budgeted people on a daily or weekly rate – is it 5/6 days?
- Editor commences day after shoot
- Be clear how many prep and wrap days there are
- Get a post-production supervisor to come in to check workflow/ budget, etc.
- Keep other casting to a minimum for extras, supporting artists
- Children need chaperones and to be driven to and from set as well as a separate resting area

ROCLIFFE NOTES on...
WAYS TO BUDGET EFFECTIVELY

- Learn how to get the best quotes and to haggle. Start off mean with the pennies.

- Budgets are ex-VAT normally but don't forget you have to cash flow this. You can only claim back VAT if you are VAT-registered, which needs to be done when you set up your company. Ask for VAT receipts.

- Do the 'worst case scenario' budget first. Spread the money wisely to give 'on-screen value'. Allow hidden pockets of contingency in some accounts.

- Remember fringes – National Insurance, holiday pay, etc. Excluding these can come back and bite you.

- Work out which is cheapest – cash, credit card or bank transfer – and which needs to be paid when.

- Cash flow your spend – work out what you need to pay out and when.

- Use purchase orders and deal memos to state the rate and the deal ahead of time. This also allows you to track spend.

- Manage the petty cash carefully – whatever you do, don't hand out too many floats, and don't allow subfloats (people giving money from their float to someone else). People are responsible for their own float. Clear each float before another is issued to the same person.

- Catering can be as simple as the local greasy spoon and friendly restaurants that do meal deals.

- Go green – ask the costume and make-up departments to go electronic and upload their continuity notes to a dropbox or email at the end of the day.

- Have a central stationery cupboard and don't overbuy.

- Remember the camera body is not expensive – it's the lenses that cost money.

- Get in touch with product placement companies who will give you free products to use as props. Clearances are done ahead of time and you must return any items you use.

- Security, insurance and drives. Hire companies won't let out kit without insurance and you may need to hire a guard to watch over equipment. You also need hard drives to store the material and as many cards for the camera as you can get.

- Some cast may agree to make their own way to the set if you are centrally located.

- Inform the crew that this will be a paperless shoot, that call sheets will be emailed and that paper copies of scripts and schedules will only be available on request. This may not work with sides, and if a crew member has a reason for needing a paper copy, make sure this is available.

- Use your own home as a location.

- Go handheld.

- Work out how much time you have to spend on pages and scenes allowing masters, singles and two-shots.

- Don't use car rigs – instead, remove headrests and film from the back and passenger seats.

- Avoid costly stunt shots by using reaction shots and sound effects in post.

- Can expensive locations be replaced with exteriors?

- Allow time to record voiceover on set to avoid ADR and use as a guide track for the edit.

....

▶ See Appendix for sample budgets

A TO Z OF PRODUCTION

Everything described in this chapter takes place simultaneously, not necessarily consecutively or in a particular order. Pre-production is the most hectic time for the production team and there are never enough hours in the day.

Working on low-budget projects is fulfilling, but it can be hard going for all involved. It's a remarkable achievement when, creatively and logistically, you come together with a cast and crew and make a filmic story in a short period of time. At some point during production, acknowledge that accomplishment and thank your collaborators.

There are a variety of things you need to know. Like a scratched record I will repeat again and again: safety first. The welfare of your cast and crew must be your priority. Never compromise that. We're making entertainment, not saving lives. As long as you're organised, keep a record of everything and don't panic, you'll be fine!

Don't be afraid to ask questions. Work with what you have. Learn to recognise the things you don't know and surround yourself with people who do.

ROCLIFFE NOTES on...

SOFT PREP ACTIVITIES

- Set up a limited company.
- Set up a bank account.
- Get legal paperwork in order.
- Create a production schedule.
- In the UK, register for a British Film Certificate (on the BFI website) in order to be able to apply for Tax Certification.
- Lock the screenplay.
- Register for VAT.
- Negative check the script for clearances.
- Get clearances.
- Break down the script.
- Create a shooting schedule.
- Create the budget and cash flow based on the locked script.
- Location scout and lock locations.
- Get lead cast.
- Get your HoDs in place.
- Agree on shooting medium/stock.
- Complete health and safety/risk assessments.
- Obtain risk assessments from department heads – lighting, grip, camera, etc.
- Set up a production office.
- Prepare a storyboard/shot list.
- Conduct pre-production meetings with HoDs and key crew.
- Hire equipment – camera/sound/lights/special effects/edit.
- Order hard drives or film stock.

- Key HoD should breakdown script and present budgets.
- Carry out tech recces.
- Have final pre-production meeting.
- Organise insurance.
- Organise camera/lenses/stock tests.
- Do equipment checks and checkouts.
- Issue production paperwork to crew.
- Find a composer.
- Book post-production facilities.

••

DIRECTOR OR WRITER-DIRECTOR PREP

Even before a film is green-lit, a director can get into the heart of it and run it in their head. The more you think about how the film you imagine will look, the more you'll see it evolving. Newer directors are sometimes scared to share how they want to shoot in case they are shown up, so create an environment where communication and collaboration are paramount to how you work.

Set up one-to-one meetings with your key heads of department. Then, early in prep, organise a scene-by-scene page turn with your line producer, director of photography (DoP), production designer (PD), costume designer, 1st assistant director and hair & make-up designer, etc. to discuss what you're thinking for each scene. This isn't a free for all but a way of exploring what you want from the script.

Great acting, fantastic camerawork, good sound and editing are all components of a good film and if done badly can ruin a great script. Get on the same page with your team and don't keep everything in your mind. Share, discuss, communicate.

FODHLA CRONIN O'REILLY: It was super helpful for the director and I to go through the scenes and work out the intention in each and what we wanted to say. Was there a possibility of conveying that in

105

another scene that already existed? Combine scenes to get as much as possible on-screen within your schedule, because it will always be tight and down to the wire – no matter how prepped you are.

ANDREA HARKIN: By the time it comes to prepping scenes I've already figured out a lot of things. The DoP and I will have discussed the shooting style, the aspect ratio, the type of movement we want, the type of lighting and the quality of the image. We share visual references. We watch a lot of clips and look at images and discuss ideas, coming up with a visual approach. Share ideas about how to apply this visual approach to the scenes. You don't get through every scene, and some scenes don't require it as they're very much about performance, but to do this kind of thinking ahead has helped me enormously on the day. So, once I have an approach with the DoP and a location, it comes down to the scene thinking about performance beats, narrative beats, blocking and the shot list. The first few things have already been done in some way as I've spent time casting and (hopefully) rehearsing and offering script feedback to the writer. I will already have a sense of the key performance beats and narrative beats of the scenes. As I may need to recall these things , I will make notes on what I need to achieve on the floor. Once I've figured out the blocking (either in advance or on the day), the DoP and I will look at how to cover that scene with the camera angles/shots. I refer to the shot list I've often done the night before. Then it's about concentrating on the performances. I have a small template document that I fill in the night before for each scene. I print it out in A5 and attach it to my sides. It contains the story point of the scene; any technical notes (copied/pasted from a spreadsheet I've prepared during prep and based on conversations with the DoP); the character's info – where each character was last seen, and where they are now on their emotional journey; the last line of the scene before this scene; the first line of the scene after this scene. This helps orient myself and remember where we are in the story (which is necessary when shooting several episodes out of sequence), and also serves to remind myself of the key story beats and how it will cut together with what comes before and after. It can be time-consuming but this preparation and having a template help.

ROCLIFFE NOTES on...

DIRECTOR'S PREP

- It all begins with the script. This is everyone's starting point. Work out how you connect with it.

- Is there a specific style in mind? Is there an overall look?

- What films do you like the look of that you want to replicate?

- Sit down and plan how you're going to shoot each scene. Make notes.

- Think about what happened before and after to each character in the scene.

- Watch films with your DoP and production designer and discuss shots and approach. From this will come your shot list.

- Nothing beats a table-read rehearsal prior to the shoot if you can manage one. Have one-to-one time with your actors – discuss each part and what you want from it.

- Create bonding games. Rowan Athale sent all the guys in *The Rise* out to play golf together. Don't be afraid to throw the shot list away if you want to try something else.

- Plan any action or special-effects scenes – don't leave them to chance on the day. Consult with stunt coordinators and special-effects teams about what you want to achieve and let them suggest the safest and most time-effective way to shoot the scene.

- Have meetings with your HoDs where you talk through what it is you want them to bring to the table. The more briefs you give your HoDs, the closer they can get to giving you a refined idea of what it is you want.

- Ask make-up and costume to prepare look-books and reference ideas for each of the characters at crucial points in the film. They are visual artists let so let them show you what they think the character looks like based on your brief. If their brief doesn't match up, tell them, communicate.

- Recce and visit locations to plan how you will shoot the scenes. Edit the film in your head.

- Make your mind up, make choices. Decide specifically what you're saying at each moment.

....

A BASIC SHOT LIST

There will be multiple setups or different angles during a scene, usually shot with multiple shots/takes from each setup. Each shot is the positioning of the camera and lighting (as decided by the director and DoP). A great book on this is *Film Directing Shot by Shot: Visualizing from Concept to Screen* by Steven Katz.

It's fine for a director to explain how many angles are wanted on something, but work with your team. Perhaps your 1st AD may tell you certain shots may take more time because they require new lighting setups. Work together to come up with a solution as this can eat up 30 minutes of your shooting day. Together with the DoP, gaffer and 1st AD you may find a quicker way to get what you need as a team. Asking for help doesn't mean you don't know what you're doing and won't be seen as such.

It's always tempting to get lots of angles on the scenes you love and then hold back on those that are maybe not as exciting. If you spend too long on a particular scene it will take longer and you will run out of time.

Don't shoot the same thing the same way over and over again. Do you need to run the scene from the top for each take when you know you have the coverage in the edit?

The ability to adapt and compromise is a gift in any director. It is also a skill which comes with experience (also known as learning the hard way). Instead, try something a different way, and shoot it both ways if you're torn between the two. When an actor wants to try something different get it your way first and then let them try it.

When something isn't working, change it. Similarly, don't make things too self-evident; it's almost like you're forcing the audience to get it when they probably already have!

The pace of a film is very hard to judge on set and you can feel in the edit suite when it's too slow. Always try doing a take with a faster pace or more energy.

If a producer feels strongly about giving a note on a story beat, the extras or a moment, they should do so quietly and respectfully. This is not a personal criticism; however, it is not an invitation to jump up every five minutes with suggestions between takes – that's not fair, and director and producer should be respectful of that process.

This is a very simplistic breakdown but you also need to work out how you're going to frame the shot:

- Single shot of the entire scene called the master of the scene from start to finish, from an angle that keeps all the characters in view. It is often long shot and can also be your establishing shot

- Single on each of the characters speaking

- Shot by shot in the order of the edit for an action/visual sequence – usually storyboarded

- Two-shot

- Coverage or reaction shots on characters

- Cutaways on physical action, including the rooms

- Breakdown of how long you're going to spend on each scene by shot and time on each shot

Shot sizes will vary:

- ELS – Extreme long shot
- LS – Long shot
- MLS – Medium long shot – knee to head
- MS – Medium shot – waist to head
- MCU – Medium close-up – head and shoulders
- CU – Close-up
- BCU – Big close-up
- ECU – Extreme close-up

A PRODUCTION TEAM

A good production manager or line producer knows their stuff and has the contacts to make things work. Contrary to popular opinion, they are not all about telling you that you 'can't have' something – rather, their primary objective is to make a budget work and stretch to accommodate the scale of the project effectively.

One of the first things they'll do is create a before-production schedule to show how much time is left before shooting and what needs to be done. The one thing people won't forgive on a production is bad planning. The production schedule goes from prep through to final delivery and differs from the shooting schedule, which lists the scenes.

Often, the producer of a low-budget film will do this before starting.

SAMPLE FEATURE FILM PRODUCTION SCHEDULE

Pre-prep	6-10 weeks	Set date
Prep	4 weeks	
Shoot	4.4 weeks	
Edit	10 weeks	
Post	12 weeks	
Delivery	2 weeks	

Week Commencing	Shoot week	Meetings	New starters
Soft prep	**Prep week –8**	Lock script – neg check script Contact talent agents re: HoDs Contact actors' agents	Director Assistant coordinator
	Prep week –6	Set up meetings with HoDs – LP, 1st AD, DoP, PD for one-to-ones	

Week Commencing	Shoot week	Meetings	New starters
	Prep week −5	Castings Meetings with DoP to break down script Concept meetings with PD Recce any locations with DoP and PM Booking camera Scene-by-scene meeting Meet with stunt coordinators and special-effects people to discuss what is needed Get any child licences sorted	Production designer PM DoP
	Prep weeks −4 to −3	Book crew Contracting Set up accounts with costume, prop stores, equipment-hire companies Post-production quotes Casting secondary roles Insurance Getting accounting system in place Special-effects team will liaise with 1st and 2nd assistant directors, stunt coordinators, production designer, armourer, make-up designer, costume designer and DoP Workflow meeting with editor, DIT, post supervisor	

Week Commencing	Shoot week	Meetings	New starters
	Prep week −2	HoD meeting Recce Meeting with make-up Meeting with costume Camera and lense test	1st AD DoP Costume designer Art director Standby art director
	Prep week −1	Rehearsals commence Costume fittings Make-up test	2nd AD Props master Cast arrive All HoDs
	−2 days	Prep, recce Load in camera Load in lighting Load in grip Load in costume Prep walkies	
	Shoot week 1		
	Shoot week 2		
	Shoot week 3		
	Shoot week 4		
	Edit 1	Return of kit and props	
	Edit 2	Begin paperwork delivery assembling	
	Edit 3		
	Edit 4	1st assembly screening | feedback	

Week Commencing	Shoot week	Meetings	New starters
	Edit 5		
	Edit 6	2nd assembly screening | feedback	
	Edit 7		
	Edit 8	Fine cut	
	Edit 9	Final-cut screening | changes	
	Edit 10	Picture lock	
	Post 1	ADR, VFX, foley, music	
	Post 2	Sound effects/pre-mix	
	Post 3	Sound effects/pre-mix	
	Post 4	Sound effects/pre-mix	
	Post 5	Sound effects/pre-mix	
	Post 6	VFX and music delivered Final mix	
	Post 7	VFX dropped in | clean-ups	
	Post 8	Final mix	
	Post 9	Conform | grade	
	Post 10	Grade – DCP created Quality check (QC) DCP	
	Delivery	Deliver final film, technical and paperwork	

ACCOMMODATION, PER DIEMS, TRAVEL

No matter when your production has to travel it costs money to accommodate, feed and per diem everyone. Whilst you can try to crew locally, you may not have the contacts or connections – contact the local film office and ask for their list of crew. Hire a local production manager (PM) or production office coordinator (POC) with local knowledge to help set up the production.

On bigger films there is someone who looks after travel and accommodation. In the lower-budget bracket, however, production will look after this. A sizeable chunk of your budget will go on any travel and accommodation and this is money not appearing on-screen. Avoid where possible having to travel cast and crew, or travel only essential crew and hire locally, particularly on low-budget films. Is there a way to shoot closer to the city?

On *Chicken Soup*, a short I directed, with good lighting and a good production designer we made an allotment in East Finchley look like a remote Libyan farmhouse.

The production will be expected to cover accommodation, travel and per diems. On *Scouting Book for Boys* we stayed in a caravan park; no one minded – it was fun. A friend stayed in a YMCA. Professional casts and crews will make allowances but expect cleanliness, comfort and some will want their own room and shower. Don't expect anyone to share without agreeing this in advance.

....

ROCLIFFE NOTES on...
TRAVELLING CREW

- Hire a local PM or POC with knowledge of the area.

- Contact the local film office for hands-on advice on accommodation, crew and locations.

- Find local crew and keep those travelling to a minimum.

- Explore cheaper options and negotiate a group rate with a hotel or B&B. Get breakfast included as this saves on meals – reflect this in the call sheet.

- Airbnb is great but you need to provide breakfast.

- Check the theatre 'digs' list or crew rooms on social media.

- Book as far in advance as you can and check the cancellation policy so you're not out of pocket if dates shift.

- Per diems are overnight allowances for crew to pay for meals. BECTU and PACT have set rates. Either pay for people's meals or give them an allowance.

- Travel includes trains, boats, planes and taxis. Book as soon as you know your dates but, again, check the cancellation policy in case dates change or something is cancelled.

- With cast bookings, dates change so do buy flexible tickets.

- Consider hiring a minibus plus fuel instead of trains when the journey time is between one and four hours.

....

ACCOUNTS

Keeping on top of your accounts. This is essential on a film. You must keep track of your spend. There are ways to be environmentally conscious and save money. Make sure you get weekly cost reports during shoot.

On very low-budget films I've also worked with Moneypenny and Sargent-Disc, which takes the worry away as they handle the cost reports on what you have spent and what you have left to spend.

I've also had accountants work on films part-time, which means the onus is on the production department and line producer to stay on top of the accounts. This can go very wrong so keep a vigilant eye on things as it's very hard to go back over accounts at the end.

ANNA GRIFFIN: On a tight budget you have to squeeze as much as you can out of each line. If this means chasing the fivers, so be it. Don't go with the first quotes you get – haggle, negotiate. All those fivers will mount up and make a difference. Always get post-production advice way before you start shooting, so you know what you need, in what format you need it and how much of it you need to make the post house's job easier. If the film is delivered to the post house and it's complicated for their workflow, it will hurt.

BUDGET

This details what you have budgeted to spend.

CASH FLOW

This tells you the projected spend per week, which can help keep you in credit. Cash flow should also include VAT costs, so you know where you are.

COST REPORTS

These tell you what was budgeted and how it was spent. They show how you're doing spend-wise and the variation between what you had to spend and what you've actually spent, as well as what is left in the budget.

....

ROCLIFFE NOTES on...
ACCOUNTS

- Invest in a good accountant or package – even someone with bookkeeping experience who can add things up correctly.

- A producer should be looking at the cost report – what's been spent and what is left to spend.

- If you overspend in production you may not have money for post, or you may be forced to stop the shoot.

- The art department, costume department and make-up department will need cash floats to buy in advance of the shoot.

- Use a payroll company for payroll, to navigate the complexities of National Insurance, pensions and student loans. It costs a little more but may save you money on penalties you might incur if you make a mistake.

- For amounts over a certain figure, have the producer and accountant/line producer act as double signatories.

- Manage the petty cash carefully – don't hand out too many floats or give people pre-paid credit cards.

- Don't allow subfloats (one person loaning money to another). Each person should be responsible for their own float.

- Clear each float before another is issued to the same person.

- Use purchase orders for hires, stating start and end date and delivery and collection costs.

- Be mean with the pennies and say NO a lot or ask people to justify expenditure.

- Work out what is cash or credit card or make a bank transfer if possible.

- A cash flow helps you see what needs to be paid out and when.

- Use purchase orders and deal memos to state the rate of something and the deal ahead of time.

- Check that every receipt is a VAT receipt.

- Don't spend the contingency until shooting has begun.

- Directors may say 'take it out of my fee'/'I'll pay for it later'. This tends to be forgotten later and isn't good practice.

....

ART DEPARTMENT/PRODUCTION DESIGN

The production designer is responsible for the visual look of the film. This process begins with the director, producer and production designer meeting to discuss concepts and production requirements and look at what is needed.

The director, director of photography and production designer work together to create the overall look and concept of the film. Try to get them together as early in the process as you can. They work in tandem with one another and liaise with key staff in other departments, such as lighting, costume, hair, make-up, special effects and locations, to establish a cohesive and distinctive visual appearance for the film.

With low-budget filmmaking you may not be able to afford a full art department with a full production design and construction team, but a good production designer can help unify the look of the film. Personally, I believe the strain of working with a low budget can fall heavily on the art department. Communication and management of expectations is key.

ROCLIFFE NOTES on...
DESIGN CONSIDERATIONS ON A LOW BUDGET

- Look carefully at what's in the budget to determine what's feasible and what isn't. There is both freedom and limitation for a design team on low budget as they have to work hard to create what the director wants.

- Get them to break down the prop and set list – see what you can borrow or bring in from your own home.

- Bring them on as soon as you can – people need time to buy or find bargains.

- They will need time to dress the set and this will take time away from the shoot if it doesn't happen the day before.

- Keep receipts and return as much as possible.

- What props are mentioned that a character uses, i.e. 'hand props', and what are larger props or set decoration, such as a chair or table?

- Building a set is costly, so the ideal is to find a 'walk-in or dressed' location. Adjust the script if needed as it may not be exactly what the director has in mind.

- Ensure you have time to bring the props and set together. Is what you need available at the time you need it?

- Always look for alternatives. Be resourceful and find other means of portraying what it is you need.

- The most minimal crew I've had in an art department is four – a designer, one on the live set, one setting up for the next day, and one out buying and returning. It's tough as they are prepping and striking on the job. You can do with less but you'll lose time on setup.

- Get in touch with product placement companies as they will give you free products; props and clearances are done ahead of time. Factor in the costs of returning these items. Companies will ask for a synopsis and a list of who is in the film.

- Allocate time after the shoot to return items.

- The art department may need a van or car and storage space.

••

CASTING PROCESS

Attaching talent is difficult and there's no science to it. Casting for low budget can be tough but you shouldn't limit yourself. Remember though this tends to happen after you have a fully formed script and on a low budget you will need a director, if not producer, attached. The concept of casting without a director will ensure you pretty much fall at the first hurdle. Actors want to know who will be directing them. I personally believe that as legitimate a form of approach as possible is recommended, i.e. via an agent or casting director. If you're working with a casting director, they will draw up a list of actors for each of the parts and make the approaches to the agents. Set a date or a month when you think you will start shooting, which can be six or nine months away.

One thing I encourage in filmmakers is to avoid being specific about gender or diversity unless it's essential to the story or role – that way you can cast great actors of any gender or from many different backgrounds who are reflective of society around us. You don't need to raise a giant flag to this but you do need to look at how society is portrayed in your casting choices and what you can do to make these as reflective of today as possible. There are so many reasons why cast come on board and it isn't always because of the budget.

SHIRLEY HENDERSON: I'm attracted to projects for different reasons. The story and the character are what I am keen to find out about and then I am looking for a feeling, a clue, a sense of something in the character that intrigues me and makes me want to jump in there to see what it might become. It can be that a director has sent me a script and it's someone I respect hugely, someone I have never worked with before and really want to or someone I don't know but like their chat and sensibility. Low-budget projects mainly come to my attention through my agent. Most writers send them to me that way. Occasionally someone approaches me at the very early stages for a chat about an idea they have or the early stages of a draft they might want me to read when money is just being raised and a project is not actually green lit yet. This sometimes can happen at a film festival. Sometimes it's just a chat over coffee. Sometimes it will be that I have worked with the director before and they just ask if I'd like to be part of their next film. The decision is rarely about how big the budget is.

SEAN BAKER: When you're street casting you need to find someone who is good with the public and knows how to approach people and not be intimidated.

MANON ARDISSON: Casting is a key element because your low-budget movie probably doesn't have a lot of effects and stunt sequences. On *God's Own Country* we were lucky enough to work with Shaheen Baig and Layla Merrick Wolf, and also with a Romanian casting director, Domnica Circiumaru, who found Alec. Our cast, Gemma Jones and Ian Hart, were on board with the limitations of the budget as well as filming in story order in bad weather and on a working farm, even though they'd both worked on bigger productions.

MAXINE PEAKE: When I sign up to a project the budget doesn't come into it. The script and creative team do. I'm usually drawn to lower-budget projects because there's a bravery in their storytelling and, more often than not, a larger artistic freedom. I like the idea of rolling your sleeves up and 'mucking in'. I really enjoy the element of collaboration within them. There's usually a reason a script is produced on a lower budget. One is it may not be that great (although we've all seen regular, big-budget drivel!). The other, and the reason I will attach myself, is that the story isn't mainstream commercial fare, therefore more exciting and far more fulfilling.

STEPHANIE LAING: Get the cast you want. Be strategic, be very strategic. Don't be afraid to aim high and only work with the best casting directors who share your vision but challenge you to think outside stereotypes. I chose the best, Sherry Thomas, whom I had worked with before and trusted implicitly with *Irreplaceable You*, my first film as a director.

JONNY PATERSON: With *Halfway* we were still casting the film during production. We knew we had one very important role to fill and that the character would be required during the fourth (and last) week of our shoot. We ended up casting that role with only a few days to spare before they needed to be on set. That was challenging for me on many levels.

RAY PANTHAKI: As a filmmaker, casting is everything. Because of the money involved in film, a lot of people will want a say, but listen to your gut because it's the single most important decision you'll have to make.

ADO YOSHIZAKI: We spent far too long chasing cast that were just too big for the film and holding on to every little crumb that meant we might get that person in the end. Projects need momentum, otherwise they die slowly, and your energy and motivation dies slowly too, so the least amount of time you can spend chasing cast the better. I prefer to lower the cast's star power and the budget and try to finance the film within a much more realistic framework. Keep moving, keep pushing and be creatively sure of the cast you wish to assemble. Films don't necessarily need big star names. *Victoria*, *A Girl Walks Home Alone at Night*, *Theeb* – these are all great films without any star names at all. It proves that the lower-budget indie space doesn't revolve around cast, but quality – and word of mouth.

GEOFFREY AREND: For me, the most important thing is story/character, then actors, then director. If the script is good, it's enough to get me interested. I have to want to see it. In the old days a good script and decent role were enough to get me to do it. Now I know how hard it is to pull off a good indie, so who the other actors are has become a crucial condition. The quality of the other actors is so important because you'll be spending 20 days in (probably) crappy conditions doing the work, so having great collaborators and great writing is the key to staying sane. It's also why the director is last on my priority list. If the script and actors are good and the director is bad, you still have a shot. Any other combo doesn't work in my opinion. Unless you're improving it with killer actors and a killer director, I guess. I wouldn't know as I've never done a project where improv was the intention. The Duplass brothers have definitely proven that it can work.

ROCLIFFE NOTES on...
CASTING

- Start with the script – write a list of all the characters and their characteristics. Are there any special skills needed such as driving or riding a horse?

- It's helpful if the writer, director and producer put together brief character breakdowns/descriptions to get agents and cast excited about the roles/project.

- Create the casting briefs in advance and not at the last minute!

- Have an idea of the actors you'd like to cast in each role.

- Don't dismiss or stake all your wishes on a famous name – yes do aim high but give yourself options. Many teams offer to 'stars', only to be kept waiting ages for a response and let down at the last minute.

- Talk with agents about who is up and coming and who can carry a lead. Consider actors who have made a good name for themselves in theatre or TV.

- Check the availability of your preferred choice of actor by calling their agents – this is done by a casting director or the producer.

- For more established actors, you may have to offer them the role rather than asking them to audition.

- Part of the audition may involve discussing the character's role within the story – be prepared to answer these types of questions.

- In a casting session, put the actor at ease; have someone other than the director read the other lines.

- When casting, if you can't find the right actor, rewrite the part for an actor you love. They will bring something very different to the role but equally right.

- Don't offer the actor the role immediately during or immediately after the audition. Wait until you've seen everyone.

- Give each part a meaning. Cameos can really make a film – you're more likely to get a known actor for one day than the entire shoot.

- Avoid generic titles such as Man 1 or Woman 2 – actors prefer a name.

- Don't expect the audition to be camera perfect – see how the actor responds to the character and any notes the director may have. It gives the director and actor a chance to discuss the role.

- Casting your friends can be hit and miss.

- Street casting takes time but can yield incredible results.

....

CASTING ANIMALS

Choose the animal you wish to work with and consult with an animal handler. If in doubt, check with the RSPCA. The welfare of the animal should be your priority. Work with a registered animal handler.

CASTING CHILDREN

It's really important to remember that children are children first and actors or your characters second, and appropriate behaviour should be adhered to at all times. Check the regulations of each country regarding children. In the UK it takes between four and six weeks to get a Children's Performance Licence organised and you need to apply to the local council. Children need to be driven to and from set and have a separate rest area. Chaperones are required (these can be their parents). There are strict rules governing the hours children can work on a given day and the time they must stop filming. All this needs to be fully explored and factored into the budget – it doesn't matter if they're your own children or your niece/nephew. In the UK, working with child performers, actors and supporting actors is regulated by the Children (Performances) Regulations 1968, which applies to all children from birth to the end of compulsory school age.

WORKING WITH ACTORS

PHILIPPE LIORET opened my eyes to the power of conveying emotion through silences. He got the actors to perform really emotional sequences by positioning a camera at each of them and getting them to run the scenes to each other, just thinking the lines and emotions. The results were more powerful than the scripted words. He also had great reaction shots. So find an action that reveals the character's thought process.

SHARON BIALY: It's important for actors to relax, and walking into an audition room with a casting director or director makes an actor feel very vulnerable. I liken it to them walking into my home, and it's my job to make them feel at ease. I always introduce myself, and the director and producer if they're in the room. I ask the actor if they have any questions or whether there's anything I can explain, and I usually say, 'No matter what, we're going to do it more than once.' You get one for driving here – so let's use your instincts on the first take and we can 'play' from there.

SAUL DIBB: It's about painstakingly casting the right person in the first place. After that, it's less about rehearsing the lines again and again and making them 'perfect' than it is about looking at the big picture. It's more about trying to understand that person, so you can access whatever you need in order for the actor to be able to inhabit the part in a way that line readings don't deliver.

SHRLEY HENDERSON: I find in the end there is no difference between the low- and big-budget film once the camera starts turning. The moment has arrived and it's just about trying to create something from nothing. Tell the story in the best way you can – some days you can feel comfortable, some days you feel nervous and some days it's all beyond your control. Just see what happens. Rehearsals are often a luxury in film. Most times it's just a conversation. It depends on how difficult the scenes might be, how character driven they are, whether the character is based on a real person, and whether the director likes rehearsals or not. There are no set rules. It is usually the director's call in my experience. Sometimes I hope for rehearsals and we don't get any and sometimes it's better if we just let the filming day happen in its own way. Often if improvisation is involved it's hard to rehearse anyway. Then it's more about becoming the character before you ever get to the set so that you can play freely on the day. Different jobs need a different type of beginning.

JOHN MADDEN: Find the language the actor uses, as it were, and approach each actor differently. My own personal belief (I'm talking about working on film here as opposed to the stage) is that you're unlocking a character. If you cast accurately or sympathetically, meaning you see in the actor's audition something in their make-up or approach to the part, like they are inhabiting that role, you can use the role itself as a means of communicating with the actor.

DANNY HUSTON: Were I to ask you a question about the character and you floundered or didn't know the answer, hadn't formed an idea, etc., it would ring alarm bells. It would mean you either weren't connected to the material or couldn't substantiate what you wanted to make. We actors can be cautious. Directors can get too involved with mood drawings or visual ideas. Fascinating that you're going to use a handheld style, but that doesn't tell me how I should approach the character. Actors are looking for keys to the characters.

RAY PANTHAKI: On set, be adaptable. Every actor is different and needs a different approach, but as a general consensus I think setting a tone of honesty and encouraging suggestions is a safe starting point. Also, make sure you offer the same attention to day players who may not have had the benefit of rehearsals. They are coming into this more nervous than anyone and that can often be forgotten, but it's these smaller elements that make up the bigger picture. Fortunately, I get to look at this from both perspectives. As an actor I think it's really important to be on a set that is safe. What I mean by that is an environment and relationships, particularly with the director, that are communicative, open and honest. A place in which we can be vulnerable and feel comfortable enough to suggest and try something different. Sometimes the moment takes us to where rehearsals didn't and I think it's important, providing the piece allows it, to be confident enough to be present to that feeling and act on it without fear. It's those instinctive, unplanned moments that often end up being the most memorable, but we have to be comfortable enough to go there in the first place. Once you've got your actors, rehearse. I like to consider the character on the page only a skeleton. The flesh, fat, organs and muscles are the layers I want myself and the actors to build up during rehearsal, using that time to figure out what the actors' own vulnerabilities might be and weaving them into the genetic make-up of the characters we're forming.

ANDREA HARKIN: The first thing for me is reminding myself – what is the point of this scene? If I only had time to capture one key story beat – what would it be? What is the emotional temperature of the scene? (Refer back to any notes you made at the script and reading stages.) Then – thinking about movement and energy. How do I want to block this scene with the actors? I like actors to have autonomy and make choices and I like to watch them make these choices and steer if necessary. But I also have to have an approach to blocking that makes sense in terms of the emotional temperature, the energy or movement required, the scenes that have come before and after, etc. So I'll have a couple of options up my sleeve as to how to block the scene, and one strong favourite, and if the actors do something different that works, then that's great (I quickly rearrange my shot list in my head!), but if they do something and I think my idea might be more effective, I'll ask them to try it. They are always happy to collaborate and I find it's this meeting point of offering creative freedom to actors regarding movement in the scene, but also steering and discussing and getting to the right decision, that gets the best results. If it's a dinner-table scene, obviously it's much more straightforward as there's no blocking as such. It's about choosing where to place everybody in terms of family/group hierarchy or relationships or eyelines.

···

ROCLIFFE NOTES on...

WORKING WITH ACTORS

- All actors want to give the best performance they can.

- A director should speak with an actor quietly and respectfully and tell them what they need.

- Don't hide behind the monitor; be on set, and watch. Use playback to see how the take has played out. Shoot the rehearsal. It is recommended not to play a scene back to the actors, except if it is a particular action.

- Don't overload actors with notes but don't be afraid to try out different things. It's hard for them to remember everything at once.

- Make sure to plan with the 1st AD how much time is needed for each shot.

- Allow actors to move within a scene. In black and white films there was a lot of movement that wasn't necessarily driven by the camera.

- Rehearsals can feel like a luxury but even a few hours a day or two before the shoot gives the director a real chance of talking about things that may eat into a shooting day.

- There's so little time on set. So shoot the rehearsal. People may complain but it could be the best performance and technical issues won't matter.

···

CATERING

One of the most important things to plan on a set is how to feed your crew. There are different ways of doing this. If working with your friends, it's acceptable for people to pay for themselves but if people are working for free and professional they will expect to be fed both breakfast and lunch. Food plays a massive part in the working day – an army marches on its feet. You need to buy everything in advance.

Be careful with snacks on set. Try to eat as healthily as possible. People always complain about the weight they gain.

••

ROCLIFFE NOTES on...
CATERING ON BUDGET

- Check dietary requirements in advance with cast and crew for vegetarians, vegans or allergies.

- Breakfast is served half an hour before unit call.

- Lunch is 5 or 5.5 hours after unit call and should last one hour.

- Crew may agree to 'food in hand' or less time over lunch, but you must agree it in advance – with every crew member.

- Tea, coffee and water should be provided all day. Write names on bottles/cups and get people to refill.

- Keep a supply of fruit, biscuits and chocolate to get through the day – buy in the markets or pound shops.

- Local greasy spoons can provide breakfast rolls including vegetarian options.

- In remote locations I've brought a kettle and toaster, and provided milk, cereals, fruit, yoghurts, jams, butter and bread.

- Do a deal with a local restaurant.

- Give everyone a meal allowance (cash in hand) to buy their own lunch, which they sign for.

- Don't forget the offset crew who also need lunch.

- Pizza and fish and chips are great low-budget filmmaking choices but they have to be eaten immediately or they go cold.

CONTINUITY

It's a false economy not to have someone keeping track of what's been captured on camera or 'in the can'. They list the preferred takes and shots you have as well as which scenes are left to film. Continuity and script supervision are not to be underestimated. Something Marnie Paxton-Harris mentions below made me realise that perhaps, because their role is to point out mistakes, newer filmmakers are reluctant to see their value as it makes them feel undermined. However, in actual fact, the continuity or script supervisor is the director's right-hand man/woman and best friend.

MARNIE PAXTON-HARRIS: We keep track of what's been shot and make sure everything that needs to be shot is shot. We refer to the script as to what is supposed to be shot. We record changes that are made as we shoot. We help make sure things will flow and work in editing. We catch problems and errors. We follow the story and make sure it is adhered to and that there are no conflicting situations. We offer ideas, suggestions and options. We are the producer and director's eyes and ears, the editor's advocate. We constantly keep in mind the whole story being told. We are there to assist in making the best film possible. We are a department all on our own. A huge part of the script supervisor's job is to spot mistakes so they can be fixed while shooting rather than afterwards, which is much costlier. As this boils down to telling people what they did wrong, it leads to the role being undervalued. The reality is, each mistake on its own may not be noticed by an audience engrossed in an amazing story, but if there are many little mistakes, slowly that audience will lose the ability to suspend its disbelief.

COSTUMES

Designers aim to enhance a character's personality and create an evolving plot of colour, changing social status or period through the visual design of garments and accessories, all within the boundaries of the director's vision. A designer breaks down the costumes for each character according to how many days there are in the story (story days) and how many costume changes each character needs within each day.

There are four main options for sourcing costumes. They can be a) pulled via a costume-shop stock, b) rented from a costume supplier, c) bought, or d) made to order (the most costly option).

In terms of purchasing, the costume designer usually needs double their budget to shop and procure clothing pieces; they will then return the rest to come in at budget, so appreciate this in your cash flow. They need to have enough options to try on actors and often don't have enough time to do many of their returns until the last few weeks of filming.

WHITNEY ANNE ADAMS: Designing indie films presents many unique challenges and tests the limits of what you're able to accomplish, but the fun comes from working within these constraints. You often surprise yourself with what you're able to accomplish. I'm forced to be more resourceful and usually find more interesting pieces. I also love the tight-knit crew environment that comes with a small team of passionate filmmakers who want to make the best possible film they can, no matter how many hours it takes. I'm always happiest when I'm surrounded by like-minded artists. Indie films are extremely tough but the most rewarding in the end. It takes more time, but if you're on a low-budget project, have your designer focus their time in thrift stores and consignment shops and online resalers like Etsy and eBay, as there are always a lot of hidden treasures there for not a lot of money. It may take extra time to find items but it's always worth the search.

ROCLIFFE NOTES on...

LOW-BUDGET COSTUMES

- The costume designer should be connected with the actors as soon as possible to talk about the characters and specific costume pieces so they have enough time to procure proper costumes for them.

- Get actor sizes as soon as possible so that whoever is buying/hiring costumes will have enough time to source properly fitting clothing. The ideal is to get actors to try on costumes before the day they film, otherwise you may be faced with costume problems and no time to fix them.

- Check with the costume designer – do they have their own stock of costumes and what can they bring for free or a low kit-rental fee?

- Call other productions that are finishing up in your area to see if you can get racks, hangers, rack tags, garment bags, etc., from them for a low price, or even for free, as they are usually trying to offload them. These items are necessary for any film regardless of budget and size.

- Try to connect with indie fashion houses or large fashion brands to get free merchandise that can be featured for a credit. Many brands do this for the publicity, depending on the content of the film. Most fashion brands will only want to provide clothes if there's a celebrity in the film and if the characters wearing the clothing won't be doing anything nefarious in the script.

- Costume houses will need deposits and insurance and may want to run a credit check before clothing can be taken from them. This can be a pain if it's left till the last minute.

- If the film has a contemporary setting, ask the designer to speak to the cast about their own clothing. Actors may be prepared on a low-budget film to bring some of their own clothes for free or, if you can afford it, a small allowance.

- Discuss how clothes will be washed and dried – this can add an extra two or three hours to the end of the day. If you're not working with an official wardrobe truck, someone will have to go to a laundrette or do the washing themselves at home, which can account for many hours of overtime.

- If a character is wearing the same outfit throughout the film, they will need several multiples (dupes) of the costumes, which can be cleaned and rotated. If there are stunts in the film, you will also need multiple dupes of these clothes, to allow for items getting dirty or being destroyed. Three to six repeats are usually enough, depending on the stunts.

- If you're filming outside, minimise costumes by using one coat – hats and scarves can show the changing of time and enable money to be saved on larger items. Regardless of budget, have warming gear for the actor (outer coat, hand warmers, gloves, etc.) especially if they're going to be exposed to the elements for an extended period of time.

- Uniforms are very expensive and so are hires, so take that into account when reading through the script.

....

DIT, EDIT AND WORKFLOW

The digital image technician (DIT) is the person handling the rushes. The data or rushes are the most important part of the film so you need to know they're being handled well and with care. If the drives become damaged or lost you may lose the footage.

For a variety of reasons, the rushes may not look good, and this may be worrying, especially if you don't have enough footage. It's hard to watch the rushes back, but the producer and director have to do it. It is standard practice for the DoP, and the costume, make up and production designers to see the rushes so they can watch for continuity.

ROCLIFFE NOTES on...

WORKFLOW

- Before the shoot, the editor, DoP, DIT, sound recordist, producer and post-production team discuss how the data workflow will happen. Particularly when you're working with a low budget, with little manpower, it's vital this happens correctly. Do you need to shoot in 4K or above? Is everyone aware of what aspect ratio you are shooting, what frames per second (24fps or 25fps)?

- If cards are being used, ensure they're backed up from the source card twice, not transferred across from one drive together. Experience has taught me that if the data on Drive 1 has been corrupted and you transfer from Drive 1 to your backup Drive 2, you will have two corrupted files with unusable data, and you'll have deleted the master files, so no more footage! Transfer from Card 1 to Drive 1 and Card 1 to Drive 2 – BACK UP EVERYTHING FROM SOURCE.

- Sometimes the data will need to be transcoded.

- The editor will take the digested material and organise the footage or clips into bins according to scenes and angles and sync the sound.

- They will read the notes from the script supervisor with the director's preferred takes.

- At the end of each day the producer or PM or DIT takes home a copy of the rushes, with a different drive going to the editor. No drives should be kept together overnight.

- During the shoot the editor will put the rushes online (securely, via password-protected sites) for the director, editor and DoP to see.

- Costume and make-up may have to view the rushes for continuity purposes.

EQUIPMENT

Be resourceful and innovative. Hire companies are very open to doing deals with newer filmmakers, as long as you can demonstrate professionalism, i.e. you're fully insured and have a decent team on board.

SEAN BAKER: With *Tangerine* we were given a very small amount of money to make it. We had so little money we knew we wouldn't be able to pull it off, so we had to look at places to cut costs. That started in the camera department. It just so happened that, at the end of 2013, there had been some wonderful technical advances with the iPhone that allowed you to shoot HD video, as well as a tool called FilmicPro and an anamorphic adapter, created by Moondog Labs, which allowed you to shoot in true scope. These things allowed me to shoot on an iPhone in a very cinematic way. We decided to embrace the iPhone and see what it brought us in terms of benefits. It allowed us to shoot clandestinely and work on the street without calling attention to ourselves. Our footprint was small, our presence was small, and if you'd seen us from across the street, shooting, you wouldn't have thought we were shooting a film. The biggest giveaway was the boom pole. This all started as an alternative way of shooting due to budgetary constraints; however, it quickly became part of the aesthetic. For me, it's always important that the medium complements the content and vice versa. It's not about shooting on a camera that's cheaper and faster; it's about using that device to enhance your content.

ROCLIFFE NOTES on...
EQUIPMENT HIRE

- Create a tech spec sheet with aspect ratio, format, frames per second, etc.
- Check the equipment list against the supplier's inventory and the kit against the inventory.

- The smaller the packages, the more portable the production. You also need to be aware what the post-workflow/route is, as each new camera differs.

- Camera – set up camera tests at the facilities house. Test **ALL** your equipment before you leave the rental houses and check you have everything you need. I've had it where the wrong head was sent with the legs (tripod) and we couldn't use it. Don't assume it's all there – to do so could well make an ass out of you. Check what's there against what you requested. Get a tripod or legs – tall and small. Try out different shots in prep. Think about how you're composing the shot. The camera package is put together by the DoP. Should your DoP have their own camera, all the better, but to hire in lenses can cost as much as hiring a whole kit. You want a full package with lenses, clapperboard, etc. Handheld is cheaper but does it suit the movie? It needs to be done well and enhance the film – you don't want to give the viewer motion sickness.

- Sound – a good sound team can save you a fortune in post. They will usually supply their own kit and transport for a fee. Speak to them about how many radio mics they have, etc. Schedule and record any voiceover or off-camera dialogue on set so you can cut it into the edit. You can state that this is guide track for later.

- Grip package – you will have dolly and tracks. You'll need manpower to carry and move these.

- Lighting – do you need a generator to run the lights and do you have sufficient manpower to run them? Many gaffers have kit you can hire. Use available light where possible. Bring gaffers along on recces to see what you need.

- Consumables – don't forget that sound and camera departments use consumables (batteries, tape, markers, etc.).

- Decide which are the money shots and put the money into those.

- Do deals with HoDs on their personal equipment.

- Cost up getting equipment delivered and returned on the day. This can be more cost-effective than carrying it around for the duration of the shoot.

- For tracking shots, look at alternatives – wheelchair, skateboard, dolly, rather than big equipment.

- Minimise the number of walkie-talkies.

- Go paperless (email call sheets) and keep a small printer for sides (A5 sheets of script dialogue for the actors), but keep printing to essentials or requests only.

- Ask editors if they can supply their own kit.

- Always factor in delivery and collection costs and note when kit is due back.

- Do a final sweep of the set/location at the end of each shoot day for bits of kit.

• •

HARD DRIVES

You need hard drives to store the material you've shot. You'll also need as many cards for the camera as you can get, as you will use these up quickly depending on whether you shoot 2K, 4K or higher. The higher the K, the more drives you'll need. The editor will also need to back up all the cuts.

INSURANCE

Many insurance companies are super helpful about working out your needs – e.g. Aon, Entertainment Vision Sound Insurance Brokers, Integro, Media Insurance Brokers, Quartz, WK – so shop around for the best deal.

There are four types of insurance you'll need:

- Public and Private Liability – protects the production against claims by the public and/or organisations for damage/injury sustained during the course of filming. Check out the price of annual versus single-policy insurance and always ask about excess charges (for claiming).

- Employers' Liability – a legal requirement for a company if you have a limited company and are engaging people.

- Equipment Insurance – all hires will expect equipment insurance to be in place (and will ask for proof). Without this you'll have to take out insurance with the hire company and this can be more costly.

- Errors and Omissions (E&O) Insurance – indemnifies producers against lawsuits arising from the content of a production, including those alleging (a) infringement of copyright, (b) libel or slander, (c) invasion of privacy, (d) plagiarism or unauthorised copying of ideas, (e) defamation or degrading of products (trade libel), and (f) infringement on title, slogan or trademark. Any type of production may be eligible for E&O insurance. It must be obtained BEFORE distribution, not after the fact. Productions that have had prior losses due to content errors are not eligible for coverage.

As stated above, hire companies won't let out kit without insurance. Cameras and other expensive equipment need to be stored somewhere secure at night, usually with a person present. Leaving these items in an office is not considered secure. Check with your insurance provider what their terms are; if equipment isn't supervised overnight you may find you're not covered. So, as the producer, expect to take home the camera and a copy of the rushes.

A production may be insured, but this doesn't mean a runner driver with their own car is insured to take an actor. Unless it is a 'hire car', taxi or has special business insurance, which covers a privately owned car being used for business, it isn't covered. On a low budget, you may agree with the cast that they make their own way to the set if you're centrally located. Bigger names, children and older cast members should be driven by taxi. Similarly, if an actor can drive but doesn't have a full driving licence they are not insured to drive a car.

LOCATIONS

Choosing a location can be as involved as casting. Sometimes it can be super frustrating when what you see in your mind's eye may not be available, or exist, or be practical in film terms.

ASIF KAPADIA: Don't rebuild a location to fit your script; change the script to fit that great location. It's all about being flexible and making sure you use what is in front of you, rather than spending lots of money changing what you have; using something great that you find will bring more to the project. You may write something that climaxes in a cathedral but, when you go to find the cathedral, stumble across a beautiful tree. That tree is your cathedral, a natural one. So you change your script to fit with the tree and film there. You don't have to have lots of money to change things that aren't key to the story. Know when to be flexible and when not; know the crux of the idea behind why you want to make this film and keep that close to your heart. Write it down on top of your computer, on your wall.

ANDREA HARKIN: By the time I am prepping scenes, I have usually found the main locations already. I find there isn't much point prepping a scene in any visual detail or in terms of blocking and shot listing until you have the locations. But I know other directors work differently and might storyboard or shot list in advance. Sometimes you have to do that if you're having trouble pinning down a location. But usually the location will tell you how to shoot the scene. It will offer opportunities and restrictions. Sometimes a location is chosen based on backdrop or visual appeal and therefore the blocking of the actors also has to take in that view or that motivation for choosing the location. Usually the motivation can be found for the actors to make this work as well. And also the choices have to work from a lighting and shooting perspective, so if the DoP watches the blocking rehearsal they can advise if it's going to be difficult or time-consuming to shoot or if it needs a rethink. Often, a respectful DoP won't want to get involved or interrupt this rehearsal process, but they'll watch so they can get ahead with thoughts about lighting and shooting, and then we have a quick heads-together before the crew rehearsal to run over the setups, which is very valuable and saves time in the long run.

SEAN BAKER: Always be polite and respectful. These people are going out of their way to help you for free or for very little, so never affect their business or their property. Sometimes you can get a location for free by simply being polite and connecting with the owner. Communication is key. Maybe you grew up in the small town you want to film in or have similar interests. Keep a small footprint and clean up after you are done. You have to embrace your limitations and look for the benefits, avoiding the drawbacks you can; that's when you get the most out of things. On *The Florida Project* we had a helicopter always around the hotel we were shooting at, so we made it a character and it became an integral part of the movie. Even when something looks like it's not going to be a benefit, it can enhance your film.

FODHLA CRONIN O'REILLY: Make sure you're shooting rather than simply moving between locations. Spend as much time on camera as you can and keep location moves to a minimum. Your performances are key, so time spent with the actors is what matters most.

• •

ROCLIFFE NOTES on...
LOCATIONS

- Start scouting for locations as early as you can.

- Choose a location that is going to give you great production value.

- Avoid paying in full for locations in advance. Put down a deposit, because they may insist you pay more on the day.

- Think carefully before offering your own home as a location. I personally wouldn't have a large film crew in my home. That said, the crew I've worked with have always been hugely respectful.

- The owner, not the tenant, must give permission.

- Don't decide on a location before camera, sound and design have seen it.

- Is there enough space to shoot in and move around?

- What is the power source?

- How far away is the location from public transport?

- Where will the unit base be?

- Are there toilets, changing facilities, a cast holding area, kit prep area, eating area?

- Are there clearance issues – graphics, signs, shops you need to clear?

- Are you using the location during the day or night – have you visited it during the hours you will be shooting?

- What kind of art dressing will be needed?

- Is this a public place? Do you need permission from the police?

- If this is an exterior location – what have you got as rain cover?

- How will you make good the location after the shoot?

- What backup location have you got in case this one falls through?

- Location wet-downs look lovely but cost a fortune as you have to pay for the water and keep the path/road wet. DoPs and directors love them because they look so nice. Yes, they do. Be innovative or hope it rains beforehand. If you're using water, make sure you cover all your kit with wet-weather gear.

- An actual location is better than a set build.

- Set as much of the action as you can outside during the day as it's cheaper and gives great cinematic qualities, although you're at the mercy of the weather.

- Interiors can be better for nighttime scenes as you have better control of light. A lot of interior night scenes means blacking out windows – is that easy to do or are you in a high-rise?

- Decide on a central location for the film, which doesn't necessarily mean an anonymous city. It can have a building that provides several options, e.g. a school, a house, a hospital. You're aiming to make as few unit moves as possible.

MAKE-UP AND HAIR

Make-up and hair are a vital part of the shoot. They need to work in hygienic conditions with good lighting. A make-up team usually comes with its own kit and can offer a box rental. You will need a minimum of two make-up and hair artists as it can take up to 25 minutes per character to get camera ready. This isn't just about making someone look good but having their skin be right for their age or lifestyle. The most expensive part of the day is the shoot, and not having enough people in make-up will slow you down.

There is a whole world of skill and experience here – wigs, body art, bald caps, moustaches, beards, prosthetics. Prosthetics are used on an actor's face or body in order to change their shape and appearance. This can be as simple as adding scars or wounds, or more complex creations such as noses, chins and foreheads.

SHANNON THOMPSON: Tip one... hire early (hair and make-up often come last and have to make make-up and hair magic happen in a limited amount of time). We often don't get the prep time to create the look the way we should. Two... no matter what, always do a camera test with lights and wardrobe. It will save you so much time, money and drama. Three... listen to the team when they say they need a specific amount of time to create the look. Don't rush us if we say we need 20 minutes; let us have that time. If the actor looks good or realistic, it will last and be talked about. Lastly, trust your team! You've hired a professional to help you create what you envisioned.

SAFETY/SET MEDIC/HEALTH AND SAFETY

A set medic is required when riggers, lighting and construction teams are building something or when there are stunts and special effects. You need to carry out risk assessments and have a health and safety advisor come on the recce. Similarly, you'll need safety boats when you have divers, and lifeguards when you have actors in the water. Safety is no accident

STUNTS

When it comes to stunts, allow enough time to set up, rehearse and shoot. Planning and rehearsal are essential. Consult a registered stunt coordinator and send them the script or scenes with stunts. Arrange a meeting and discuss with them the best approach and most time- and cost-effective ways to shoot those sequences. They will advise if you need a double for the actor or if it is something an actor can safely do. It's vital that no risks are taken with stunts. No actor or crew member or member of the public should be at risk. You need to visit the location where the stunts will be performed and check what equipment is required.

You may need to inform the police or fire brigade and have a nurse or paramedic on set. Avoid scheduling stunts at the end of the day – never compromise safety to save money or time. Never let a child do his/her own stunts.

Double-check when an actor says they can drive, ride, swim, etc. You need to carry out certain health checks and they need proper licences, i.e. full, not provisional, driving licences, PADI licences, flying licences.

PETER PEDRERO: I have three things I tell everyone. A: Don't assume, just because somebody has been recommended as a stunt coordinator, or they have told you they are a stunt coordinator, that they are qualified to do the job. Check with the BSR. B: Don't *believe*, always check. If the stunt coordinator is legit, they will have spent years performing stunts in order to become a stunt coordinator. Stunt coordinators have showreels of their exploits built up over a period of time (years). C: Check everything: a CV is only proof of a production credit, not a person's ability to carry out a stunt correctly and with the right safety precautions in place. Contact a producer on one of the shows. Employing a stunt coordinator without the relevant experience happens for monetary reasons – but you need to employ someone who has the skill to do the job safely. The reason for employing a BSR stunt coordinator is that they have *5 years'* minimum experience of orchestrating their own stunts with no other artist involved. Simply put, it's the difference between drivers with provisional and full licences.

> BSR is the British Stunt Register.
>
> Check with your insurers as they may require you to have a registered stunt coordinator on set if you are carrying out any stunts. Without one you may not get insurance.

ROCLIFFE NOTES on...

STUNTS

- Ask a stunt coordinator to advise at script stage what can be achieved within your budget.

- Check with your insurers as most will insist on a coordinator for insurance purposes.

- Make-up and costume will also need to be involved so that the double resembles the actor if they need a wig or costume fitting.

- Guns will require an armourer. If the gun is fired you'll need ear protectors for everyone; you can't have guns on the street otherwise. If bullets are being fired, you'll also need to have special effects involved. And you must let the police know if you're filming with guns.

- Consider falls – slips, stairs, trips – as stunts. Anything involving falling from any sort of height will require railings, harnesses, airbags.

- If you're filming cars or bikes, you'll need action vehicles and camera-tracking vehicles and equipment. You may also need stunt drivers.

- Even a simple punch is a stunt and should be discussed with a stunt/fight coordinator, as should any type of fighting that includes swords, riots, armed guards, mobs, etc.

- Water involves divers and safety boats and equipment as well as wetsuits, life jackets, etc.

TRANSPORTATION

On a low budget, it often falls to the production to organise most of this.

You'll need some form of transportation and specialist vans for dollies, tracks, lighting, etc. It's dangerous to overload your vehicle and there are legal limits with hefty fines.

Sometimes you have facilities vehicles – make-up and costume, honeywagons.

Generally, the art department, costume, camera grip, and lighting will all need some form of transportation to get them around. You can get deliveries on a day-to-day basis but this can be tricky if you are moving around a lot.

UNIT BASE

This can be someone's home or a spare office. Such spaces can be difficult to find but ask around. I find local pubs often have vacant upstairs rooms. These can also double as dining/holding areas to avoid facilities trucks (honeywagons, dining buses, artists' trailers).

I've used Airbnb apartments/houses to accommodate actors, costume and make-up, but always make it clear to the owners what their property is being used for.

VISUAL EFFECTS

There are specialised companies that create visual effects. Normally you send the script to a visual-effects supervisor within a company and they come back to you with a breakdown and costs, as well as a risk assessment. You also need to enquire how long it will take. Then you schedule a meeting with the producer and director to find out how you can achieve what is required.

You may find on a lower-budget film that many of your special effects won't be feasible and so you will need to adapt accordingly.

You need to check that the special-effects company will provide safety equipment. Get them to send an estimate, too, and outline overtime, travel, transport, etc. This can be costly so do keep some contingency for extras in special effects.

A special-effects team will liaise with the 1st and 2nd assistant directors, stunt coordinators, production designer, armourer, make-up designer, costume designer and DoP. A meeting with the director needs to be scheduled in prep, before shooting any special effects, to discuss how everything will work.

....

ROCLIFFE NOTES on...

DIFFERENT VISUAL EFFECTS

- Blue or green or model or glass shots
- Special equipment for falls
- Prosthetics or specialised make-up
- Blood
- Blood moving
- Animatronic animals or monsters
- Remotely controlled devices
- Fires
- Models
- Builds – these are specially made props or dressing, such as a suitcase that springs open
- Wirework – things that move using wires, which are then removed in post

- Props that are devised not to hurt anyone during a stunt, e.g. a rubber spade or knife
- Doors and walls that people fall against or through
- Vehicles crashing/exploding
- Wind machine
- Rain machine – these need bowsers (water containers and a water supply)
- Snow machine
- Smoke machine
- Dry ice
- Explosions
- Limbs/body parts

....

08

CREWING UP

There are many ways to go about finding your crew. Contact talent agents and ask who is available. It's a question of cold calling. They will want to know the rate and dates, but they may also have clients who want to do a film or drama.

Ask around if you have friends in the industry to see who they recommend.

Look at film schools such as the NFTS, etc., for recent graduates.

Do research: watch films and read the credits. Make a list of who you like, then google them or look them up on IMDb. Many key HoDs have websites.

Write to them directly and explain what you like about their work and why you'd like to work with them. DON'T suggest they can jump on your coattails to success, especially when their careers are already established. If they aren't available, ask if they can recommend anyone.

Advertise on social media outlets for HoD crews and ask for CVs and showreels. Emphasise that they must have credible credits.

Before you approach anyone, you need to be prepared to answer the questions crew across the globe will ask:

- When are we shooting?
- What's my department's budget?
- How much prep time have I got?
- How long is the shoot?
- Is it a 6-day or 5-day week or 11-day fortnight?
- Is it a 12-hour or 11-hour day?
- Are we shooting over weekends?

CREWING UP OR FINDING CREW

Of course we all want to work with the best crew possible and that does save a lot of time and money. You'll be surprised how very experienced crew will help out on a short or low-budget feature, if they like you and the script. Put your ego to one side – this is a collaboration not a dictatorship.

You want to find people who can help you realise your vision, so make sure you know what kind of film you want to make. Understand that you are now making a film to be a professional, so understand the dynamic of a film crew – just because things are done a certain way you don't understand, that doesn't make them wrong. If you seek to hire professionals, don't think they won't see through your lack of experience.

Don't advertise, in general terms, for a sound person, or an art-department-type job. Know what people do. Grips aren't just manual labourers – gripping is a highly skilled job that involves moving the camera in a controlled manner. If you're clear about what you want to achieve with the project, you'll be in a good place. This goes for directors and producers. If people believe in you and your vision and they trust you, they won't let you down. Everyone wants to be a part of something special or, at the start of someone's career, that has potential.

ROCLIFFE NOTES on...
FINDING CREW

- The best way, of course, is to get recommendations from people you know. Ask industry friends if they know of anyone who might be interested.

- Start crewing up as early on in prep as you can. Advertise on film sites. Ask for references if you need to.

- Many HoDs will have regular crew they work with.

- Check out film schools, diary services and agencies. Ask if they have anyone who is available. Someone having a quiet patch might be up for helping out new talent.

- When approaching crew, offer them an opportunity to step up. A camera assistant becomes a focus puller, a 3rd AD becomes a 1st AD. Why ask someone to do you a favour when you can give them an opportunity to prove themself at a higher-grade level and get a credit at that level. If there's something in it where they gain not financially, but professionally, that's an incentive.

- Always offer to cover travel and food!

- Treat everyone with respect – goodwill goes a long way.

- Offer expenses if you can't afford to pay someone, or a buyout or some form of payment.

- The main thing is to work with people who will challenge you, and who will push you to do better, not those who will simply be nice.

DIFFERENT DEPARTMENTS ON BIGGER PRODUCTIONS

This is what you would see on a bigger-budget film. The producer isn't a member of the production team; the line producer/co-producer is:

- Director/producers/writers
- Production
- Accounting
- Art department
- Assistant directors
- Camera
- Casting
- Continuity
- Costume
- Craft services/catering
- Editorial

- Electric
- Grips
- Hair/make-up
- Legal
- Locations
- Post-production
- Property
- Scenic
- Script clearance
- Script coordinator
- Script supervisor
- Security
- Set decoration
- Set medic
- Sound
- Transportation

BARE MINIMUM CREW

Using an SLR or camera phone, with natural lighting, minimal locations, natural make-up, the cast wearing their own clothes, and the producer and director working out a shooting schedule, this is what you might expect:

- Director
- Producer
- DoP/Camera person
- Sound person
- Art department person
- Runner
- Cast

IDEAL SMALL-SET PRODUCTION CREW – SHORTS, LOW-BUDGET FEATURES

- Director, producer, cast
- Production manager
- Production coordinator
- Location scout
- Accountant (part-time or via a service such as Moneypenny or Sargent-Disc)
- 1st AD
- 2nd AD
- 3rd AD – key for communication between set and base
- Continuity – can save time and money later on set
- Runners
- DoP/camera operator
- Focus puller
- DIT
- Grip
- Gaffer
- 1 x electrician (sparks)
- Sound mixer
- Boom operator
- Production designer/art director
- Set dresser
- Props buyer and standby
- Costume
- Costume assistant
- Make-up and hair designer
- Make-up and hair artist
- Editor

BREAKDOWN OF EACH DEPARTMENT AND RESPONSIBILITIES

Department	Role	Responsibilities
Production	Line Producer	Supervises the preparation of a film's budget and cost of the production for investors.
	Production Manager	Supervises non-creative aspects of production, including personnel, budgeting and scheduling.
	Production Coordinator	Responsible for logistics like hiring crew, renting equipment and booking talent. Generates and distributes production paperwork. Coordinates travel, transport and accommodation.
Accounting	Production Accountant	Works out cost of production, communicates with financiers, controls cash flow.
Art Department	Production Designer/Art Director	Works with director/producer to come up with the visual style and setting of the story. Production designers liaise closely with the DoP and director. They look after the design style for sets, locations, graphics, props, lighting, camera angles and costumes.
	Property Manager/Props Master	In charge of care and maintenance of all props associated with the production, making sure they are available on time and within budgetary requirements. Ensures all props arrive to the shooting location in a camera-ready fashion. During filming, maintains prop continuity between scenes.

Department	Role	Responsibilities
Assistant Directors	1st Assistant Director	Oversees day-to-day management of cast and crew, including schedule, script and the set. Creates shooting schedule having liaised with DoP, production designer, costume and make-up.
	2nd Assistant Director	Supports the 1st AD in the day-to-day management of cast and crew, including schedule, script and the set, and creates call sheet. Books extras and taxis for cast to and from set.
	3rd Assistant Director	Moves actors from point A to point B, organises extras and supervises the production assistants. He or she also has the special duty of set messenger, relaying information – usually by radio – between cast and crew members. They also hand out and return all walkie-talkies each evening.
Assistant Directors	Floor Runner	Carrying out tasks on set to help the progression of the production. Running errands. Teas, coffees.
Camera	Director of Photography	Head of all technical departments. Responsible for how the film looks visually, usually in consultation with the director.
	1st Assistant Camera/Focus Puller	Responsible for care and maintenance of all camera equipment. Pulls focus on the camera.
	DIT	Making sure all footage is secure and backed up.
	Stills 1	Takes photographs on set.
Casting	Casting Director	Organises casting/selecting actors for all roles.
	Casting Associate	Helps the casting director audition/select actors.

Department	Role	Responsibilities
Costume	Costume Designer	In charge of designing, creating, acquiring and hiring all costumes.
	Costume Assistant	Oversees the day-to-day running and use of the wardrobe on set. Gets costumes cleaned and ready
Electric	Gaffer	Head of electrical department. Works closely with DoP.
	Electrician	Assists gaffer on lighting.
Grips	Grip	Operates dolly or cranes and holds camera.
Hair/ Make-up	Hair & Make-up Designer	Responsible for designing, application and continuity throughout. Creates the look for the production requirements and oversees continuity.
	Make-up & Hair Artist	Creates make-up and hair styles to meet production requirements and oversees make-up continuity.
Legal	Production Lawyer	Creates all the production contracts.
Locations	Location Manager	Responsible for arranging everything at selected locations. Contracts/local residents, etc.
	Location Scout	Searches for suitable locations.
Post-production	Post-production Supervisor	Reports to producer. In charge of delivering the film on time and within budget.
Editorial	Editor	Works closely with director to edit and finish the film.
Script Supervisor/ Continuity	Script Supervisor	Keeps notes on what has/hasn't been filmed and any changes made. Shots and lenses used as well as preferred takes by director.

Department	Role	Responsibilities
Sound	Sound Mixer	Records the sound on set, makes sure dialogue recorded during filming is clear.
	Boom Operator	Holds the boom and works to capture the dialogue.

SCREENSKILLS

ScreenSkills is a UK industry body which empowers the creative industries to develop skills and talent, helping businesses to grow. They help manage investment from both industry and government to ensure the UK remains a world leader in creative talent. They also help train the next generation of creative professionals through mentoring schemes such as Guiding Lights, and by offering bursaries to support training through international partners like Rotterdam and the Berlinale. https://www.screenskills.com/

Trainee Finder is an online matching service where ScreenSkills seeks to match you and your company with new talent in the film industry. Trainee Finder provides companies with a contribution towards a trainee's cost-of-living training allowance, 50% for production placements. They are seeking to help foster new talent in lots of different companies and film productions – whether big or small, new or established.

SCREEN TRAINING IRELAND

Screen Training Ireland, part of Fís Éireann/Screen Ireland, is a unique resource for the Irish screen industry, offering training by professionals for professionals. It is committed to providing customised, state-of-the-art training to support the development of Irish screen sectors. The Creativity and Creative Collaboration training strand focuses on providing development opportunities to creatives. It places storytelling and the unique voices of Irish creatives at the heart of what it does.

Screen Training Ireland provides emerging talent with the opportunity to meet and collaborate with experienced practitioners, creating a cohesive means of progression for emerging talent, and new creative approaches for established practitioners. It offers development opportunities for screenwriters, directors, actors, creative producers, programme makers and visual creatives, aiming to provide emerging talent with exposure to key creative trainers on a national and international level. For more established talent, the aim is to provide a less structured approach where new ideas and the collaborative creative process can be explored. Screen Training Ireland also supports international training through their bursary award scheme, enabling experienced Irish professionals to participate in training opportunities on the international circuit and, where necessary, design a development opportunity customised to meet their individual needs.

www.screentrainingireland.ie.

PAPERWORK

LEGAL CONTRACTS

When I started making short films I didn't realise the importance of contracts, particularly option agreements and writer agreements. I touted *No Deposit, No Return* at Cannes to raise money without realising the writer could have taken it back at any time and my effort would have been in vain. Unlikely as that was to happen, I really should have had an option agreement or shopping agreement in place, without which I had no legal attachment to the film.

A contract isn't something to be scared of. It should simply serve to iron out all the elements of an agreement and then be forgotten about unless something goes wrong.

An entertainment lawyer will do a package deal for you and you should always consult one. They will charge you a fee to cover the entire production, providing you with the right legal support. It is recommended that, before you start working with a writer, cast or crew, you seek legal advice and sign contracts. Verbal agreements aren't worth the paper they're not written on.

Legal advisors will give you templates for all the contracts you need. When it comes to the complex world of financing, sales and marketing agreements, they will understand the language involved and help you get the best deal. It's a massive support to have someone like this in your corner.

There are useful templates, drawn up for general information purposes, in *The Guerilla Film Makers Handbook*.

LIST OF MAIN CONTRACTS USED

DEVELOPMENT

- Option and assignment
- Shopping agreement
- Treatment agreement
- Interview agreement
- Writer's agreement

PRODUCTION

- Producer's agreement
- Director's agreement
- Actors' agreements
- Crew agreements
- Loan-out agreements
- Location agreements
- Composer agreement
- Musician's agreement
- Stock footage agreement

FINANCING AND DISTRIBUTION

- Executive producer agreements
- Completion bond agreement
- Financing agreements
- Interparty agreement
- Sales agency agreement
- Distribution agreement
- Collection agreement
- Exhibitor agreement

NEGATIVE CHECK/SCRIPT CLEARANCE/LIBEL READ

At the script stage, producers try to avoid referring to characters or companies that might be confused with real people or institutions.

They do this by conducting what's known as a negative check. All the names of fictional characters, places, phone numbers, etc., are researched to see if they actually exist and, if they do, alternatives are suggested. The primary reason for this practice is to prevent any possible legal action for libel, which could arise as a result. Errors and omissions insurers will want to see a copy of this report.

CLEARANCES

Clearances begin with understanding copyright, and the laws vary around the world. An original piece of work belongs to the creator. Everything requires a clearance or the right to use it. With writers, directors, actors, extras and crew, sign contracts allowing you to use their work and image. Without these rights the film cannot be shown in public.

With images or brands, contact the owner company and ask for permission, which must be done in advance of the shoot. If clearances aren't obtained, you must change names, avoid using real numbers, create your own graphics and logos, and turn props around so the labels aren't seen.

Write to companies and ask for permission. All filmmakers should keep a log of clearances and the relevant documentation. Sometimes companies or individuals will ask to see the scene or script pages to understand the context.

You need to clear:

- Artwork – including branding, paintings, logos
- Book covers – which is why an art department will create book covers
- Stock footage on TV
- Shop fronts, commercial premises and certain locations
- Vehicle licence plates
- Logos – computer logos, phone logos
- Dialogue/spoken references – organisations, brands, names of real people
- 'Fair use' – a legal term usually applied to news and documentaries

PRODUCTION PAPERWORK TRAIL

This is not a definitive list but a guide. Templates for these can be found on the internet.

Document	What is it?	Who sees it?
Budget – top sheet	Summary of budgeted spend by department.	Producers, accountant, line producer, financiers, bond, insurers
Budget – detailed	Detailed line-by-line spend by department.	Producers, accountant, line producer, financiers, bond, insurers
Call sheet	Daily overview of what scenes are being shot, call times, location, weather, emergency numbers and main contact numbers.	Issued to everyone
Cash flow	When spend is projected.	Producers, accountant, line producer, financiers, bond, insurers
Cast list	List of cast photos with their name and character.	Anyone
Confidential cast list	Photos of cast list with their personal details, including addresses, phone numbers and emails.	Need-to-know basis, usually going to director, 2nd AD, coordinator, PM, costume and make-up
Contracts	Cast	To the individual/agent
	Crew	To the individual/agent
	Extras	To the individual/agent
	Locations	To the location owner
	Music	To the composer/publisher/rights holder
Cost report	Shows what you have actually spent compared with predicted spend.	Producers, accountant, line producer, financiers, bond, insurers

Document	What is it?	Who sees it?
Cast day out of days (Doods)	Shows the actors' daily schedule.	Cast, ADs, make-up, costume
Location list	Lists the locations and scenes and sets filmed at that location.	Anyone
Movement order	How to get to a location – parking, nearest police station, hospital, emergency details and a map.	Everyone
Risk assessment	Showing the health and safety precautions needed.	Everyone
Petty cash request forms	Requests for float.	Anyone – on request
Reconciliation forms	Reconciles expenses with what has been spent.	Anyone – on request
Progress report	A report on the shoot day's activities. This shows what was shot, data used, lists any accidents, visitors to set, additional crew on that day, specialist equipment hired, amount of extras, and amalgamates the individual department report.	Producers, accountant, line producer, financiers, bond, insurers
Continuity report/script supervisor report	A detailed record of the camera settings, the acting, audio and picture quality of each shot and changes to the script. The scenes shot, takes, and director's preferred takes. It also lists camera turnover after unit call and after lunch.	Editor/production
Purchase orders	This is an accounting document that shows when an order has been placed, whether it is a rental or purchase, and how long it is rented for. It also lists the delivery address.	Accounts, supplier and signed off by line producer

Document	What is it?	Who sees it?
Schedule – strip sheet/ one-line schedule	A shooting schedule listing the scenes to be shot day by day with cast numbers and a brief summary of each scene.	Everyone
Schedule – expanded	A detailed shooting schedule listing the scenes to be shot day by day.	Everyone
Unit list/ contact list	A list of crew, their phone numbers and email addresses. It used to list home addresses but this is less common now.	Everyone
Suppliers list	List of all suppliers by company name, with contact addresses, phone numbers, emails.	On request
AD report	Assistant director's report – listing cast pickup, arrival and departures. Turnover times. Scenes shot and dropped. Compiled by 2nd AD.	Production
Camera report	Camera department's report.	Production/editor
EDL	Edit Decision List contains information from the editor about what footage is used.	Post Production
Sound report	Sound report – notes on takes, etc.	Production/editor
DIT report	Digital report and log of all the rushes.	Production/editor/DoP

COMMON TERMS USED IN FILMMAKING

- Breakfast – first meal of day before call time
- Call time – time you are required on set
- Copy (that) – I understand
- Dressing – furniture on a set
- Leads – main actors
- Location – where you are shooting
- Lock the script or the picture – not making any further changes to the script or edit
- Lunch – main food break in shoot – regardless of when that happens
- Overtime – time worked over and above the working day
- Pre-call – an early call before breakfast/unit call
- Pre-prep – soft preparation before official prep begins
- Prep – preparation for the movie or pre-production
- Prop – is short for property and is anything handled by an actor
- Recce – a trip to a potential location
- Reshoots – scenes from the film that need to be shot again
- Pickup shot – shots that are done after production, during the edit, to help the story
- Supporting artistes/extras – crowd or extras
- Strike time – time allocated to taking down the set
- Turnover – start of filming
- Turning – filming
- Turnaround – break between wrap at end of day and unit call
- Unit call – time you are called to set
- Watch your backs – someone is coming behind you
- Wrap – time you finish shooting

POST-PRODUCTION AND DELIVERY

More often than not, the area we know the least about, underbudget for and underestimate is the post-production period, which could almost be considered rebuilding the film from scratch. You don't need to know everything about post but you do need to find people who know what they're doing. It's very important to contact post-production companies at the earliest possible stage of prep and get quotes, and then budget accordingly – not after a film has been shot. The concept of 'fixing it in post' is an indulgence you can't afford on a low budget as it won't have been accounted for.

Schedule, prep, meet, discuss progress and give feedback at every stage. Agree the amount of feedback rounds you will have.

CAMILLE GATIN: There are always deals to be made – meet with lots of different companies early on before the film is made.

DOMINIC BUCHANAN: Making lower-budget films is about ensuring you have enough money for post, striking the right deals with reputable people and knowing that if you go with a big post house you won't be truly prioritised when they are busy. Of course, this is subject to people's relationships. Also, you should have a post supervisor if possible.

IAN BONHÔTE: Don't underestimate sound design and the time it takes or VFX if you have any.

CHRISTINE HARTLAND: You should never work on a feature without a post-production supervisor; however, until now I've never managed to have a line in the budget for one. Post-production can be a very technical phase and can be tricky or lead to unnecessary expenses if miscalculated, so the best option is to employ someone who knows what they're doing!

CARISSA BUFFEL & KEVIN MATUSOW: We've been fortunate enough to have several great post-production partners who've been willing to work for very little money; but again, like talent, if you can make the process as painless as possible for them, that can be key to getting them on board, which means being organised and efficient when it comes to the post process. Also, cultivating relationships with up-and-coming talent in editorial, VFX and sound is paramount.

ELEMENTS OF POST-PRODUCTION

The following can commence during the edit but cannot be finalised until you have picture lock (i.e. until you have finished editing the film):

- The Assembly (see section on The Edit for definitions) – happens during and straight after the shoot and is done by the editor.

- The Edit – usually a certain amount of time is contractually agreed for the 'Director's Cut' before anyone else gets involved.

- VFX preparation can commence before the shoot; however, it is hard to create them during the shoot, edit and even before picture lock as you don't know how they are being used in the film. Certain pre-planned shots or asset builds can commence before picture lock. It is important not to turn over any VFX shots unless you are positive they will end up in the final film or your costs will spiral and money will be wasted.

- ADR – additional voice recording, which can commence around or after picture lock.

- Foley – sound effects commence around or after picture lock.

- Sound editing – dialogues, effects, including Foley and ADR commence around or after picture lock. Same with music composition and recording and mixing.

- Rerecord and mix – the sound and layers – must be picture locked. There is the pre-mix and final mix.

- M&E mix – music and effects – must be picture locked.

- Titles – title, main, end roll (must be picture locked). You should determine whether the main titles will be at the beginning or end of the film and mock a draft up as soon as possible, especially if they are part of a front-title sequence. Assembly of titles begins in wrap week by the production manager. This can be built up during post.

- Conform and grade film – must be picture locked.

- DCP – Digital Cinema Package – the final film, which cannot be created until the film has had its grade and final mix.

- Quality check DCP.

- Deliverables – physical sound and picture deliverables as well as continuity script and legal and financial paperwork and statements.

- Delivery of final film.

A POST-PRODUCTION SUPERVISOR'S INSIGHT

VERITY WISLOCKI is a producer and post-production supervisor who has worked on a variety of budgeted productions and makes films herself. She sees them from production through the post period to final delivery. It is a very delicate period where all the balls that were dropped during prep and production have to be collected and accounted for – but, in this case, after the fact.

LOW-BUDGET POST-PRODUCTION TIPS BY VERITY WISLOCKI

- NEVER, EVER say 'We'll fix it in post'! Do everything possible in camera otherwise it will cost you a fortune.

- Planning, planning, planning! Make sure you plan your shoot properly in terms of VFX plates, archive clearance, graphics, music clearance (e.g. if you have any characters singing in the film), etc.

- Issue a 'fact sheet' detailing aspect ratio, sound and picture speeds, etc., and a 'workflow document' that includes where the rushes are being delivered, storage of backup, etc., and everyone's responsibilities.

- Make sure everyone is aware of what their responsibilities are – there are so many grey areas in film!

- Never assume someone else is thinking about or dealing with questions – always ask, especially on lower-budget productions where people may not be as experienced.

- Ensure every department is speaking to each other, get an editor/ post-production sound person/post-production supervisor/VFX crew involved pre-shoot as much as is possible, even if it's just to ask advice.

- Make sure you have someone paying attention to clearances/ what is in shot or in earshot that may not be clearable. Having to blow your VFX budget on paint-outs due to poor planning will mean you can't afford that beautiful VFX shot that would have transformed the film!

- Get your paperwork in as much order as possible during the shoot – crew, location contracts (much easier to get them signed while people are still around).

- Try and get someone to help you with a post-production budget and schedule – either a post supervisor or get quotes from various post houses, etc. Make sure you leave a realistic amount of money for post! Although this will no doubt change, to have a realistic and workable post budget and schedule pre-shoot will be hugely helpful for the film.

- Don't just sign any contract in your desperation to get the deal done without looking at the delivery requirements and making sure you have removed anything unnecessary – most of the people negotiating these contracts just use delivery requirements from years ago without understanding what is and isn't necessary, like a 35mm print.

- Don't underestimate good production sound crew – it will save you a fortune in post! Better still, ask someone who works in post sound who they would recommend. A brilliant assistant editor is essential, too, if you can afford it.

- There is so much technical lingo in film. If you don't understand anything don't be afraid of sounding stupid – just ask someone!

THE EDIT

The filming is the gathering of material and the edit is where we really see the film come together. It is a slow and painful process at times and a director often finds themselves falling in and out of love with the film until it comes together – and not necessarily as they would have imagined.

There are various stages to the edit:

- Logging – the data or rushes are ingested and logged into bins out of order and the sound rushes are synced.

- First assembly – usually crude version of the film with master shots plotting out the story.

- Second and third assemblies – more polished and refined versions.

- Usually there is feedback in between each assembly, and the editor and director will try out different takes and ideas, moving scenes and reactions around.

- Rough cut – the film is arranged in the order of the script and refined.

- First cut – this is where we really begin to see the later version of the film come in with more nuance.

- Fine cut – here the details become more refined and the pace and tone are more distinguishable.

- Locked picture – this is when the final version of the film has been agreed, from which there is an EDL (edit decision list) and quicktime made for the sound. The VFX and grade teams start work at this point.

RORY DUNGAN: When selecting an editor, which is one of the most critical creative choices you'll make on a film, absolutely talk to as many people as possible who have worked with them. Not just directors from the creative side, but also producers who may have encountered issues that are entirely uncreative. It's not enough that they've worked on good films, where it can be difficult to disentangle their work from that of the director, so it's crucial to find out as much as possible about them from other sources.

ADO YOSHIZAKI: It's probably a cliché but the film is genuinely remade in the edit – and those weeks when you are starting the edit and shaping the film are so important. It also depends on whether the film has a lot of VFX work to do or not. The right editor is so key. Put in place a structure where you get to meet a lot of editors and really get to talk to them about the film and the way they work.

VERITY WISLOCKI: No film suffers from being shorter. An Oscar-winning editor said to me, nobody comes out of a cinema saying, 'That film was too short,' and nobody is going to find the film as interesting as the director does!

• •

ROCLIFFE NOTES on...
EDITING

- Find an editor who has their own kit they can cut on (Avid, etc.). If the post house is providing the editing equipment, make sure your editor knows how to cut on it.

- Create an edit schedule and specific times for producers and writers to come in and see cuts throughout the entire edit period – these can be pushed.

- When an editor and director watch the rushes together, a director should give the editor a list of their preferred takes. A continuity person should also list them on their reports on the day.

- Start building a first assembly by using the master shot and then edit in takes from singles. Lay down a conversation in the whole and insert reactions.

- A first assembly is always slow and clunky – sound quality may not be good and the colours can seem flatter than on the day. It's like a first-draft script.

- Record any voiceover you can cut into the edit – even if it hasn't been captured on set, ask the actor to record into their phone for guide purposes.

- Don't be married to one way of cutting a scene. Move scenes around – edits tend to slow in the middle, so be aware of pace and of being over-expositional.

- Don't be afraid to bring the writer into the edit to rewrite ADR or advise on how it is holding together.

- Don't keep a scene in if it isn't working. Create an edit bin (folder) where all deleted scenes are put. Every scene in the film needs to serve a purpose and drive the film along – cut it if not. This is really painful, especially when you've had a vision or spent a lot of money on a scene or shot, but if it doesn't help the film as a whole, get rid of it.

- Put in text cards where dialogue is missing, and list pickup shots. Use guide music tracks and subtitles to fill in where VFX should be.

- Bring in VFX and sound designers early to watch edits so they can advise where you need to hold longer on a shot or if a sequence is going to need VFX plates. Mark any VFX in-progress shots in the cut so people realise they aren't final.

- For special effects, try cutting these in two shots and use actor reaction shots to cut down your costs.

- Bring in fresh eyes, even a new editor to give notes. It's tough but essentially good for the film.

- No film suffers from being shorter – 82–100 minutes is ample.

....

FEEDBACK AND TEST SCREENINGS

It's really important to get feedback. Throughout the edit you should do screenings to test audiences' reactions to the film. It can be a small group or a big group. I like to get a small group of people together as they are less self-conscious when it comes to discussing the film afterwards.

As with all feedback, some is useful and some not. Susan Jacobson described the test screening of her feature *The Holding* as being so uncomfortable she'd rather have stood naked in front of people.

At drama school our crits felt like a blood bath and deeply personal. I wanted the floor to swallow me up, but they were essential if I was to get any better. I adapted and developed thick skin. Know who to get feedback from and how to take it in. I think it's best not to try and analyse reactions too much; just take in what is said and see what makes sense.

ADO YOSHIZAKI: Speaking to other producers, I discovered the value of testing the film with friends and family (who didn't know anything about it), with financiers and, best of all, proper test screenings. Each of these testing stages was very helpful, no matter how experienced the director and/or editor. It's the audience that decides whether a film is good or not. Therefore, building in stages during post so you can show the film and, most importantly, making sure you have enough editing time left to effect any changes, is a very good idea.

. . . .

ROCLIFFE NOTES on...
SCREENINGS

- Don't start by giving a review of your film or apologising. Say it is an early cut and sound and mix are only temporary. You want to know what's working or not.

- Screening the film and feedback is essential during the edit period.

- Friends and family may not be used to the lack of grading, special effects and poor sound quality, but they will be able to tell you where they got bored, where they got confused and if the story makes sense.

- Do tell family and friends this is a safe space to speak openly, but that they mustn't tweet or comment publicly on the film yet as it is a work in progress.

- Professionals will be more understanding of the process. They will be far more tuned in to things that aren't working and ways to fix them. Whether or not to bring crew to screenings is a difficult one because they are more familiar with the work and the nuances, so may not give the best notes.

- Watch an assembly or cut of a film the whole way through – don't take notes as you watch it as you will have missed something while looking at your notes in the dark.

- If you find yourself drifting or getting restless in a cut, note that point in the film.

- If something doesn't work, try it another way, recut it or cut it out completely.

CAST AND CREW SCREENING

A screening of the finished film and a thank you to those who have worked on it. Make a list.

MUSIC

A score can elevate a film to a new level. It can also be expensive to sync tracks, so working with a composer is often the more cost-effective and interesting way to work. Consider working with a composer to score the film with opening and closing pieces and incidental music.

However, ensure you agree up front what the deal is. Usually it should be a full buyout of their services including all recording, musician, studio and engineer costs, delivery in 5.1 mix if needed, worldwide, all media in perpetuity. You also need to agree whether they are keeping their publishing rights (likely if you are offering a low fee!) or whether the production company wishes to acquire them. If the latter, then your agreement needs to include these deal terms and you will need a third-party publisher to administer the revenue for you.

Note: if you have a small budget, live players may not be affordable for your composer. And if you do use live players, they will need to sign either a buyout agreement for their performance or a PACT form, if they are members of the Musicians' Union, at their applicable rates. It's usually the combined use fee for a film buyout.

CLAIRE FREEMAN: If you have a low budget for source music it's also worth contacting music libraries and one-stop shops in the first instance as they will do a music search for you – and offer low-cost syncs on a tier basis, dependent on your budget. If you want to use commercial songs you should ask a music supervisor to help, as you'll need to clear the publishing (song) and master (recording) and potentially pay reuse fees if there are session musicians involved. An experienced music supervisor has established working relationships with all of the major labels and publishers and can be invaluable in helping you clear your track of choice.

DOMINIC BUCHANAN: Trying to clear music myself – trying to do a deal with an agent over the phone for the first time – was a big mistake (NEVER do that – get a music supervisor). Beyond the obvious reasons, you need to have everything in writing so you can have time to reflect, go over things with your lawyer's input, and for your own safety.

VERITY WISLOCKI: On most films we use what is known as a 'temp score', which can be very useful, but with low-budget filmmaking this can also be a bit dangerous if it includes tracks that will be too expensive to clear, as people can get attached to them.

ROCLIFFE NOTES on...

MUSIC

- All films can feel empty until you add music – that's a fact! Don't despair.

- Some directors put music all over the cut from day one and this isn't necessarily great.

- Speak to a music supervisor. Even for advice. They know the ins and outs of how everything works.

- Ask friends who have bands or musicians whether they have tracks they could let you use – but check they aren't signed or published.

- Contact sound recording and music colleges to see who they have.

- Explore library music and one-stop shops.

- Work with a composer to score the entire film, and ensure they have enough time.

- There has to be a continuity with the music as it can change the tone and pace of the film.

- Background music – if music is played on location, make sure it is cleared or pre-clear it.

- Incidental music is not heard by the characters.

VFX – VISUAL EFFECTS

VFX are fascinating to me as they are such a craft. They can be anything from computer-generated effects to anything that is difficult to get on camera. They can be added to live action or done by specialists through matte painting, projection, graphics, and created in a number of ways.

Painting out can happen if you have to remove things that shouldn't be seen on-screen – gaffer tape, a light, an item that hasn't been cleared, wires in stunts, crew in reflections in windows, booms and even cups!

Visual effects begin in pre-prep with obtaining a quote from a visual-effects house or freelancer. They will give a breakdown with a quote for each effect. It's also great to decide what you need and what you can lose. You can get what are called grey renders to drop into the film as a guide, to see how they work. You cannot grade the film before the VFX have been delivered and dropped into the film.

A low-budget approach is often to work with a freelancer who can create the work in a bespoke way, although this may take more time.

DREW JONES: Regardless of the budget and scale of the project, people will give you advice early on in the process; speak to a professional before you commence even at script stage. The biggest misconception is the underestimation of the amount of time things take in the digital world. There is no 'can you just' button. Pick the shots and be aware of the duration of shots – VFX are created frame by frame and the number of shots play a part in the costs. Complexity is subjective so hence the need to consult early on. Some effects can take weeks; clean-ups can be low cost but can also spiral so communication is key as discussion and preplanning can help on costly approaches and ideas. Shoot what you can in camera and don't rely solely on VFX saving the day.

ADO YOSHIZAKI: I have made two films – one with over 140 VFX shots and one where VFX were very contained. In the former, we were lucky as we had one extremely capable VFX supervisor personally making all our shots. However, things can go very wrong with VFX and costs can spiral, so having a good handle on how to achieve the VFX within the budget is a good idea.

PICTURE POST/DIGITAL IMAGE

Get quotes from post houses before you begin prep. They will ask for your deliverables list. Ask for the standard delivery requirement masters for cinema and TV. Don't cut things out without talking it through; agree extras or overrun charges.

Grading your film can really bring it to life in terms of tone and feel. It enriches the film and its world.

This includes the conform, HD grade and creation of the DCP (Digital Cinema Package), which is what your film will be delivered on. Once you have your VFX wish list it's worth going through with the grader to work out what they feel they can fix during the grade. This can save you a fortune! With the title and end roll, visual effects have to be dropped in before you create the final DCP. This should include the technical deliverables too. You will need to provide picture masters of the film on various formats and aspect ratios. Don't forget you will undoubtedly need textless!

SOUND

One of my favourite parts of the post period is the sound design.

The sound design includes the design with effects and track lay, cleaning up of sound, Foley (sound effects), and ADR (additional dialogue recording). These have to be edited, pre-mixed and then go to the final mix. A film comes together in sound.

Actors' ADR usually begins when the film is locked, or very close to locked. It is worth bearing in mind whether you have included any free days in the actors' contracts for ADR – if not you will have to pay them every time they come in, and if you record the ADR before picture lock and then have to get them in again it will be costly.

Foley usually begin before picture lock but wouldn't be recorded until afterwards. This is a good element of post that you can get a package deal on.

You will also be asked for M&E – music and effects. These are needed for when your film is dubbed into other languages and a cinema and TV mix.

CREDITS

There are several types of credits – the billing block, main titles (which can come at the end or up front) and end roll. You also need to look at the poster credit block. For opening credits, my preference is only to list the major company, production company and film title, and put everything else at the end of the film. Very few audiences stay for the credits but they are an acknowledgement of those who have worked on the film. You also need to ask at the beginning of the edit period for each company's animated logo – it's no fun getting this done at the last minute.

VERITY WISLOCKI: Draft credits, including 'thanks to' and any contractually agreed credits, up-to-date crew and contact lists with no spelling mistakes, etc. If you leave the credits to the post crew, you're leaving them to people who weren't there and don't know the crew. Get each HoD to agree the correct credits for their department – then people can have a go at them, not you, when they watch the film and see their name is spelt wrong!

> Single card credits – these are cards with only one name
> Shared card credits – these are cards with more than one name
> End roll – this is the scrolling list

OPENING TITLES – MAIN CREDITS

You can have main titles at the beginning or end, but rarely do you put them at both. Opening credits are usually company and animated logos with the film title. Main titles can go at the end or beginning and are individual titles.

The simplest order to remember – and this is typical, not obligatory – is to start with the major companies involved, which will have been agreed in advance. If you have an interparty financing agreement, or individual financing agreements, you are contractually obligated to credit before anyone else (usually the actors – check the contracts for the order). If you are doing this for the first time, really read the 'billing/credit' section of the contracts and make a document outlining what you need to do.

Be careful whose credit you connect to the main credits – if HoDs contractually have to have their credit where certain other HoDs do, you can end up with very long main credits!

On shorts, avoid the temptation to go 'A Film By'. We recommend putting all credits other than title at the end unless you have contractual obligations. It should be about people seeing the work.

This is followed by a list of the most important contributors to the film, starting with the least important, ending with the most important, in this order: producer(s), writer(s), director.

- ANIMATED LOGOS
- PRODUCTION COMPANY presents (distributor)
- A PRODUCTION COMPANY production (producer)
- Film title
- Lead cast
- Supporting cast
- Casting director
- Music composer
- Hair & Make-Up designer
- Costume designer
- Associate producers
- Editors
- Production designer
- Director of photography
- Executive producer
- Producer(s)
- Writer(s)
- Director

CLOSING TITLES – MAIN CREDITS

The main credits at the end of a film appear in reverse order from as they were at the front. The end credits start with above-the-line individuals first, and are often single or shared cards. The customary order is as follows:

- Director
- Writer(s)
- Producer(s)
- Executive producer

- Lead cast
- Supporting cast
- Casting director
- Director of photography
- Production designer
- Editor
- Associate producers
- Costume designer
- Music composer
- Hair & Make-Up designer

· ·

ROCLIFFE NOTES on...

END ROLL

- Getting the credits wrong can be costly in post production if things aren't noticed until the last minute. Check and double check contracts to ensure you don't have to remake your DCP.

- There is no wrong way to do credits but people can see when it has not been done to industry standards.

- Download software to create credits, which will also help with the order in the end roll.

- Watch the end credits of films on YouTube.

- Avoid listing a person's name multiple times in the credits. Merge the various credits into one where possible.

- A DIY version of an end roll is a PDF with an animation added in the edit.

- Check contractual obligations for cast and also on any financing agreements, including soft money lenders.

- Spellcheck the names against the signed contracts for all crew.

- At the end of the film, list your thank you credits.

- You may be required to put logos for equipment suppliers or post-production houses.

- Add the copyright symbol and year of completion.

- You need to have the end credits and end roller complete before the music track can be completed as it is timed to this.

- Check if certain HoDs have letters after their names.

- Sometimes tax credits obtained from shooting locations will require an additional logo on the end roller. Check this in the contracts.

....

DELIVERY AND DELIVERABLES

Right at the end of post-production a delivery date is set. This is when all the physical materials and paperwork are given to the financier or sales agent or distributor. All delivery begins way before, however, in the prep stage, when you must work out what you need at the very end.

Having worked my way up through production, as a coordinator, it was new to me, understanding what you needed to do in post. Never underestimate the delivery and the deliverables. This is split into two parts: paper and technical. A sales agent and distributor will ask you for all these things and some of them cost money.

Things you will get asked for that you can avoid are DVD delivery – what about on a USB stick? DVDs cost a lot to make. People often say they'll get the buyers to pay for them. Those days are gone! It's so rare on a low budget, so make sure you budget enough for your deliverables.

CHRISTINE HARTLAND: The biggest learning curve on *WMD* was the discovery we didn't have any money left to cover additional deliverables (we only had a master and backup digi-beta) and E&O (Error and Omissions) insurance, with its associated legal costs. To deliver the film there was no other choice than to borrow money from a friend of my fellow producer (paid back thanks to the tax credit shortly afterwards) and put the rest on my credit card. Not something I would ever recommend, especially as the recession was just about to kick in. Before then, I had, unfortunately, never heard of E&O insurance or seen a deliverable list for a feature film. It was a hard and costly lesson to learn!

ROCLIFFE NOTES on...

DELIVERABLE ITEMS

- All technical materials such as the masters are usually quality-checked and if they fail, they must be redone.

- Confirm with the post house that they will provide a QC report. If you need to get one done independently it will be costly.

- Contracts for all artists, HoDs, crew, extras, locations.

- Proof that the producer owns the film – chain of title.

- Director, writer, producer contracts.

- Music licences and music cue sheet – confirm who will be creating the music cue sheet. A composer agreement is different to music licences.

- E&O – Errors and Omissions policy. Your production insurance company will give you a quote. I have in the past got the quote, put the money aside and bought it when someone asked to see it.

- Dialogue list – full transcript with time codes of dialogue – needed for dubbing and subtitling. This is painstaking to do! But there are specialised companies who will undertake it for you so put money aside in the budget.

- Lab access letter – this document is from your post house, saying they can get DCPs/prints made from the neg and agreeing who is able to access certain elements. If you haven't paid your post bill they may not give you this.

- Copyright notice – check quotes with the US Copyright Office. Google Electronic Copyright Office.

- Title search and trademark report – this is usually with someone like Compumark/Thomson

- EPK – press pack with bios, synopsis, stills, production notes, poster – plan this pre-shoot! This can include a featurette about making the film.

- Billing block requirements with contractual obligations (order of cast – single or shared card, main or credit roll).

- Technical delivery – picture and sound masters of the film on various formats and aspect ratios.

- M&E – music and sound effects needed for when your film is dubbed.

- US delivery requires MPAA rating certificate but this can be added later.

- Stills will require approval from some cast, and copyright from the photographer. Actors will be asked to approve 50% of single shots and 75% of group shots.

MARKETING AND PUBLIC RELATIONS

Having a marketing and release strategy is important and can form part of your finance plan. Particularly when you don't have sales and are looking at direct distribution.

CARISSA BUFFEL & KEVIN MATUSOW: We've seen many times over that the biggest oversight (we wouldn't really call it a mistake) on films made on lower budgets is not giving your sales/PR and delivery process enough weight (i.e. money). Along with that, once sold, you need to deliver and we see that process get stretched to the limit a lot in low-budget filmmaking.

MARKETING PLAN

A marketing plan outlines how you are going to promote your film.

The things or assets you will need for delivery are as follows:

- Good quality still photos, not screen grabs – these need cast approval 50% on singles and 75% on group

- A quality trailer

- An EPK (electronic press kit) – interviews with director and key cast

- A publicist on board

- Poster image

- A press pack including production notes
- Adherence to all contractual cast obligations for stills approval/EPK approval
- A list of cast in correct credit-block order
- List of all cast and crew

Your talent should be informed of the festival(s) and premiere dates so they can attend.

If you are lucky enough to have a marketing team from a sales or distribution company on board, work with them – they know the markets really well. They think differently because this is their skillset and they can help hugely.

For self-distribution, you do need to generate a network of people to come and see the film and talk about it. The more savvy you are about the audiences you target, the better the chances of success.

STANDARD EPK QUESTIONS

For DIY EPKs, ask the interviewee to repeat the question in the answer. Decide if they are looking at you or the camera and keep this consistent across all interviews. Vary the backgrounds or black out what's behind them. Make sure you have good sound.

Standard questions to ask are:

- What is the film about? Briefly describe what FILM TITLE is about.
- What drew you to the script? How did you become involved in the film?
- Tell me about your character and their journey through the film.
- How is this role different to roles you have played before?
- What is it like being directed by the director?
- Challenges of the shoot so far?
- What has been the highlight of filming for you?
- Why should people go and see this film in the cinema?

PUBLICISTS

I first met Laurent Boye from Jazo PR in New York when working on a feature there. James Knox I have known for many years, having met him during the BAFTA screening season. They each have more than a decade of publicity experience. PR is often also something we think about afterwards, or something we have to do as part of the deliverables, but it's better to start thinking about it in pre-production.

WHAT DOES A PUBLICIST DO?

LAURENT BOYE: I handle publicity for films at film festivals (Sundance, Berlin, Cannes, Venice, Toronto, AFI FEST), entertainment companies (sales agents, production companies, financiers), talent (actors, directors) or events (inviting media for coverage: panels, red carpet, photo-ops), strategically bringing awareness through B2B (business to business) or B2C (business to consumer) elevating clients' profiles to the next level.

JAMES KNOX: I'm an entertainment publicist and have worked at Cannes, the Berlinale, Venice, San Sebastián, London, Sundance London, the Sheffield Doc Fest, and Edinburgh festivals. My job is to promote films, documentaries and TV series to consumers through the media – broadcast interviews with actors, radio features with filmmakers, trailer placements with websites and picture stories in magazines and newspapers are all tactics I use to get people engaged with a piece of content and ultimately to buy a cinema ticket, tune in or stream to their device.

WHEN SHOULD A CREATIVE TALK TO A PUBLICIST?

LAURENT BOYE: It is never too early to at least talk to a publicist, if not hire one, as the more you wait, the more opportunities you might be missing, especially when your movie gets an invitation to play in a festival. You can release news, first-look photos, trailers and scenes only once, therefore be careful with social media, IMDb, etc. Whatever you post becomes public knowledge and might be a press-coverage opportunity missed.

WHAT SORT OF ELEMENTS DO YOU NEED TO INCLUDE FOR A SUCCESSFUL CAMPAIGN?

JAMES KNOX: To help create a successful publicity campaign include: production notes giving full background information on the film, a synopsis, how the project came about, interviews with and bios for all key HoDs, filmmakers and actors, and any other interesting facts. Interesting production stills featuring all the actors in a variety of different locations doing a variety of different scenes, e.g. action, showing a variety of different emotions. Behind-the-scenes images with filmmakers and actors out of character are also essential for media to give a full overview of the movie. B Roll, aka video footage, of behind-the-scenes. On-set interviews with cast and filmmakers. You might also want to bring press on to the set so they can write features about the production of the film, which will appear in media on release. Also remember to be polite, courteous and responsive to press no matter who they are or how small you think their outlet is – you never know where they might end up in their career and you want the press to be on your side!

A PUBLICIST'S NOTES ON THE PR PROCESS

Kristen O'Brien works in Austin, Texas, one of the festival capitals of America. She has run successful campaigns for both festivals and film premieres.

These tips are based on an Austin Film Society Sundance Artist Services Workshop she gave about the role of a modern publicist and how to work with one. Kristen kindly gave me permission to publish them here.

A PUBLICIST'S NOTES ON WORKING WITH FILMMAKERS

- Publicists help filmmakers shape the message they want to convey with their film, help identify the right people to see the film, and weigh in on the messaging, images and website, making sure all of this is coherent and consistent. We put out the message to the media, whether it is media attending a particular festival or the media at large on a national level.

- Publicists may also help on the social media side of getting out the message as well as with festival red carpets and festival follow-up. The value of the indie film publicist – or any good publicist for that matter – is their Rolodex and the relationships they have within the media landscape.

- Often publicists get hired too late, with only a few weeks before the festival. Ideally, they should be brought on board two months before the festival run. (This doesn't mean they are working full-time on the project, but they can start looking at your messaging and long-lead media.) For film festivals, hire your PR before the festival slate is announced.

- The most basic materials are a selection of good, high-res film stills, so the publicist can work with the filmmakers to select a strong set of key images, and the basic building blocks of the written materials that will go into a press kit (a synopsis, cast/crew bios, credits, etc.).

- You'll need to answer with the publicist basic questions like: who are you targeting? How can this story be sold? What are the goals for the film and are they realistic? It's always good to make sure you're on the same page from the get-go.

- Line up who will be available as spokesperson for the film for interviews and check they're comfortable doing interviews? Will members of the cast be available in person or by phone for interviews? Is there a backstory to your film that should be brought forward? Maybe you received a special grant we can talk about in the media notes? Is it a transgender director or director of a particular nationality? Is there a good 'struggle' story to making the film? This way, the publicist can also plan outreach to groups that can help support and get an audience for the film.

- The price of the PR's retainer will depend in many ways on the type of film (is it a small personal documentary or a more high-profile narrative with a cast of known actors, for instance?); the festival in which it's playing (major festivals usually demand higher fees); whether a press kit will have to be written largely from scratch or just edited; the amount of work it will take to put together other publicity materials, and of course the length of the contract.

- Many publicists are paid by the hour so, if they are taking a few hours trying to pull the basic info about the film from you, this all adds up. For smaller films with shorter-term contracts and the minimum of demands fees will certainly start at a few thousand dollars at the bottom end and can go way up from there.

- Expect retainers to be paid up front if it's a one-off fee or the beginning of the month for a monthly fee.

- Don't underestimate how much work is involved in media relations and messaging for a film and how important a good publicist is.

- Publicists are there to help you prep your materials in advance of a festival premiere. They put together a solid press release and consult with the festival to make sure the film is being included in all pre-festival press, and for curtain raisers they reach out to the festival PR and marketing team to see where there may be opportunities to work towards similar goals, including knowing when to take advantage of festival marketing and PR help.

- Right before the festival you start arranging interviews, and help drive media to the screenings, as well as possibly helping bring in special-interest groups, depending on the film. Post-festival you are collecting earned media, following up with media to make sure they are getting the article out if it's a post-festival article, possibly prepping a release on any awards won or if the film sold. There is a lot to do!

- It helps to have honest assessments of the work and expectations, and know what a win looks like and what is in the best interests of the film and the team. They need to know that even if the film is 'great', there should be a story hook for the media. The media want to know WHY they should care about this particular film.

- One of the challenges for publicists is that when you have five execs telling you their different opinions or differing goals, and then add to that the publicists for individual talent jumping in to give more direction or demands, it's a lot to take on for a publicist and it helps if they know who their point person is going to be. Don't have too many chefs in the kitchen.

FESTIVALS AND MARKETS

In my last book I covered festivals extensively. They are essential to a filmmaker's network and selling a film. The festival circuit is filled with great people. It's a busman's holiday for filmmakers. You get to watch films, talk films and meet fellow filmmakers. Should your film be selected, go to as many as you can afford – smaller festivals rarely pay for your flight but they may contribute towards your accommodation. When filmmakers realise the importance of getting their films seen, they ask me about creating a festival strategy.

For shorts I recommend starting with the BAFTA-accredited festival list and Academy-accredited festival list – use Withoutabox (www.withoutabox.com) or Film Freeway (www.filmfreeway.com) as this simplifies the application process. I also use the British Council's online festival directory.

The British Council also has a list of key festivals where they can support travel with their Short Film Travel Grant scheme, run with the BFI.

For features, start with the list below for a premiere but don't ignore some of the fantastic festivals around. As I'm Irish, I will always apply for Galway, Cork and Dublin – each has its own uniqueness and I love showing a film on home turf.

SEAN BAKER: I consider the festival circuit extremely closely in order to get attention on the world cinema scene. You should travel with your film, get exposure in different countries and to other cultures. I didn't initially have a strategy but I do now, although every film has a different route, so whatever strategy you have, it may get broken. You want to get into the top festivals but that doesn't always go to plan. Many factors are at play and different things get in the way. It was inspiring meeting filmmakers from different backgrounds in other countries. Meeting like-minded filmmakers and watching low-budget films at a film festival in New Zealand sparked the motivation to make *Tangerine* – that's why the entire festival team get thanks in the end credits. I encourage all aspiring filmmakers to go to festivals and understand the festival circuit, meet the programmers and understand the politics.

MANON ARDISSON: We were very lucky in that, when we applied to iFeatures in 2014, we had written in our 'Audience Statement' that we wanted the film to premiere in Sundance in the World Dramatic Competition, and then go to Berlin in the Panorama section. Which is exactly what happened! So, yes, we had a festival strategy for the launch, and then we also had a list of other festivals where our comps had played. But I realised that, beyond the world and European premieres, if your film has been sold internationally, it's the distributors who strategise festivals in their own territories to build up to the theatrical release. The Sundance and then Berlin selections did a lot for the film, especially since we won prizes during both festivals. In my opinion, that very much increased the international value of the film, drove critics to review it and, in turn, art-house cinema audiences to watch it. Further festival selections were an amazing opportunity to build the profile of the film in each territory where it was released, and also to share it with audiences where it wasn't being theatrically released, for instance in the Middle East.

RORY DUNGAN: The Galway Film Fleadh is fantastic and great for intimate access to some high-level names. Even if you don't get a meeting scheduled with them, they're around, and it's very easy to nab them for a chat or a drink. So, in terms of access to some important decision-makers, and because it's also a great place to meet Irish producers, who in turn can access Screen Ireland finance, it's ideal. Being an Irish producer, it's our annual jamboree where we all catch up and eat, drink and be merry. And watch plenty of great films. And usually get to see the latest Irish premieres and what our peers are up to. The programmers do a really good job of scouring the world's festivals and every year I find some beautiful surprise film. They also usually manage to attract some good, high-profile guests too, so you're able to meet them in a much more casual, friendly and less pressurised setting than anywhere else.

CARISSA BUFFEL & KEVIN MATUSOW: It's really important in today's market to be able to screen your work and get it into as many festivals as possible, along with outreach and early stage marketing. Note that this all costs money.

PETER SMYTH: Cannes is the best festival, period. It seems a bit unfashionable to say it these days but it's still true. Berlin is more intimate and Toronto is cooler but Cannes is still the only festival and market everyone goes to. It can be expensive and uncomfortable and the protocol can be deeply irritating, but it's the best and most important festival and will continue to be for the foreseeable future. The most important thing is for filmmakers to know which financiers/sales agents/distributors/co-producers they are targeting and then choose the festivals where they are most likely to get the maximum face-time with those targets.

JONNY PATERSON: We world-premiered at the Dallas International Film Festival and loved it. It was really a great experience and the festival director, James Faust, is a wonderful guy who does so much for the film community who come to town. If you ever get the chance to play there, I'd say grasp it with both hands. Very filmmaker-friendly!

MASOUD AMRALLA AL ALI: Preparing a good package for your film-festival submission is a must. Every festival will ask for the same. You need the film, poster, trailer, complete information about the cast and crew, a synopsis, plus maybe the tagline and director's statement. All festivals have a brochure and will want promotional materials for the film. One of the important things we struggle with is the dialogue list. If you are screening in this part of the world, for example, we need to translate the film into Arabic for the audience. If we don't have the dialogue list, we screen the film with English subtitles (if it isn't an English film).

GRAINNE HUMPHREYS: The advice I give to filmmakers about which festivals to enter is, when looking at a festival, see what they showed the year before – if they showed a film like yours then they may be interested in your film. Be realistic – film festivals need films but they also need professionals. So do your research – don't enter a food documentary into a horror festival unless it's about cannibalism.

SARAH GAVRON: So many benefits to attending a festival – meeting other filmmakers who have become friends, mentors and advisors; expanding my sense of what cinema is.

ASIF KAPADIA: By making shorts, I started getting invited to film festivals. My interest was in foreign-language films, world cinema and the great filmmakers from around the world. It was while at a short-film festival that I realised I'm an international filmmaker. It was only by travelling with my films that I discovered this was my place – the space I wanted to inhabit. It doesn't matter if your work doesn't go down well at home – if you are turned down by the British festivals, as I was – because my films were accepted at international festivals, where they won prizes. It was an interesting lesson, that you don't have to be restricted to your home market, where you live. I wanted to be an international filmmaker. I met my first producer, Bertrand Faivre, at a film festival in France.

THINGS FESTIVALS WILL WANT

- One-line synopsis
- Longer synopsis
- Credit list
- Bios of key cast, crew
- Dialogue list
- Stills – high res
- Poster

WENDY MITCHELL'S FESTIVAL TIPS

Wendy Mitchell ran the festival screenings at the British Council and is a contributing editor for *Screen International* and a consultant for the Zurich and San Sebastian Film Festivals. Here are her pointers:

- For some films, especially lower-budget ones, you need to realise you might not get a theatrical release, even in your home territory (and that's OKAY), but you can still use film festivals to get your film seen by a lot of audiences in cinemas (in fact, many more people than a failed theatrical release!).

- Keep in mind that many festivals (not the A-list ones) will pay a screening fee and, even if it's just £100-£500, that adds up if you play many festivals. So festivals can also be a way to make your money back on a low-budget film.

- Only go to a festival when you have a reason to be there, and be clear to yourself what that reason is. The reason can vary from time to time: to have meetings, to show your film, to watch a lot of other films, to just network at parties, etc. It's tragic seeing people early in their careers who spend thousands of pounds going to a festival like Cannes for no reason, and they don't get any meetings there on the ground.

- If you're a British producer or director hoping to go to Cannes to meet the BFI execs or big UK sales companies, you really should try to have a meeting with them in London during a slow week instead.

- I can't emphasise enough how important it is to pay for great professional film stills during production. Screen grabs after the shoot aren't good enough. A photo is how your film might be chosen for the cover of a magazine, how it will be seen in a poster alongside hundreds of other film posters, how it will look in a newspaper review or film-festival catalogue that is supposed to entice viewers into picking your film over all others. It will also, one day, be that tiny little square on Netflix that people see when they're browsing. So think of various images that work for all these uses; think ahead at script stage about which day you'll need your photographer on set for key moments (and, of course, they can do portraits, too, in addition to the action).

- Always have a Plan B list of festivals. Don't ever, ever assume you're definitely going to get into your first-choice festival. A naive producer said to me recently, before his film was even shot, that it would go to Berlin because the director's short had been there. No guarantee! And sometimes even brilliant films are turned down for various reasons. And also, console yourself that sometimes going to a smaller festival means being a bigger fish in a small pond (and getting more attention and reviews), rather than your film being lost in the crowd at Cannes or Toronto.

- If you can't afford a publicist for your film (do think twice, it's always worth the money) and you are headed to a film festival, do endear yourself to the festival's own publicists. They know the local media and can help guide them to your film. And don't forget the festival programmer who selected your film, as they will also want to champion it.

MARKETS

Most film markets run annually over several days (usually around one week). Often, film markets address not only films, but also television content and other multi- or transmedia content. Film markets can be broad or specialised in scope (e.g. a film market for only documentaries versus a general film market). In Chapter 15 is a list of markets as well as funding bodies, broadcasters etc. I've added Galway to this list as it's a gem of a market, and small too, and because I love it!

••

ROCLIFFE NOTES on...

MARKETS

- Attending a film market is a valuable way to learn how distribution rights are sold and what buyers are interested in.

- Cannes is a rite of passage – go do it. You'll see great films and the business side of the industry working its arse off.

- A market is where films are sold and a festival is where they are shown. A film can also be bought and sold at a film festival.

- Some films are festival films and others are very commercial. Should you go down the festival route and have a sales agent working with you on your film, talk to them about which festivals will be good for your film.

- The festival circuit is great fun but expensive and time-consuming. It's great when you're winning prizes and generating great reviews but these come at a cost.

- Film festivals charge to enter – start at the top of the list and choose carefully, making your way down.

- There is no doubt that the very best place to present your film to potential buyers is at a film market. Distributors are there to pick up rights to films.

- The artwork and trailer will play a fundamental role in getting buyers to put deals on the table. This is the first thing a buyer will see before deciding to watch the film.

• •

FESTIVALS

Film festival entry fees can be found on each of their websites. Many programmers say they spend a lot of their time dealing with incomplete submission forms or chasing images with higher resolutions. Another biggie is the dialogue list so they can create subtitles. They need to be time coded. I've created these when I haven't been able to afford one to be created for me.

World Premiere – *cannot have screened anywhere in the world*
International Premiere – *cannot have screened outside country of origin*
Continental Premiere – *cannot have screened outside of that continent*
Country Premiere/Local Premiere – *cannot have screened in country of origin OR requests that it is city of origin*

FESTIVAL DATE	Completed max 12 months before	World Premiere	International Premiere	Continent Premiere	Country Premiere OR Local Premiere	Cannot be shown on-line/Other media
Berlinale						www.berlinale.de
Feb	X	X	X	X		X
BFI London Film Festival						whatson.bfi.org.uk/lff
Oct/Nov	X				X	18 months
Busan						www.biff.kr
Oct	X					X
Cannes Film Festival Cannes sidebars need individual entry forms and entry fee					www.festival-cannes.com	
May	X	X	X			X
Cork						www.corkfilmfest.org
Nov	X				X	X
Dinard						www.festivaldufilm-dinard.com
Sep					X	
Dublin International Film Festival						www.diff.ie
Feb/Mar	X				X	X
East End Film Festival						www.eastendfilmfestival.com
Apr	X					X
Edinburgh						www.edfilmfest.org.uk
Jun/Jul	X				X	X
Fantasia						www.fantasiafestival.com/en
Jul/Aug	18 months					X
Fantastic Fest US						www.fantasticfest.com
Sep	X				X	X
BFI Flare						whatson.bfi.org.uk/flare/Online
Dec	Within last 2 years				Priority to UK premiere	X
Galway Film Fleadh						www.galwayfilmfleadh.com
July	X				X	
Hong Kong International Film Festival						www.hkiff.org.hk
Mar	X				X	

FESTIVAL DATE	Completed max 12 months before	World Premiere	International Premiere	Continent Premiere	Country Premiere OR Local Premiere	Cannot be shown on-line/Other media
Hot Docs						www.hotdocs.ca
Apr/May	X				X	X
IDFA						www.idfa.nl
Nov	X				X	X
Karlovy Vary						www.kviff.com
Jun/Jul	X	X	X		X	X
Locarno Film Festival					www.locarnofestival.ch	
Aug	X	X	X			
New York Film Festival				www.filmlinc.org/nyff55-submissions/		
Sep/Nov	X	Only world premieres may be considered for Opening and Closing Night.			X	X
Raindance					www.raindance.org	
Sep/Oct	X				X	X
Rome International Film Festival					www.riffga.com	
Oct/Nov	X			X		X
Rotterdam International Film Festival					www.iffr.com	
Jan/Feb	X			X		X
San Sebastian					www.sansebastianfestival.com	
Sep	X				X	X
Sundance					www.sundance.org	
Jan/Feb	X		X			X
SxSW						www.sxsw.com
Mar	X				X	X
Sydney Film Festival						www.sff.org.au
June	X				X	X
Telluride					www.telluridefilmfestival.org	
Aug/Sep	X				X	X

FESTIVALS AND MARKETS

FESTIVAL DATE	Completed max 12 months before	World Premiere	International Premiere	Continent Premiere	Country Premiere OR Local Premiere	Cannot be shown on-line/Other media
Tokyo						www.tiff-jp.net
Oct/Nov	X	X	X	X	X	X
Toronto						www.tiff.net
Sep	X	X	X	X	X	X
Tribeca						www.tribecafilm.com/festival
Apr/May	X				X	X
Venice						www.labiennale.org/en/cinema/2019
Aug/Sep	X	X				X

SALES COMPANIES

FILM SALES

I've included a section on sales companies to help clarify what a sales agent does and whether you need one. Most low-budget films don't have sales attached before the film has either had its festival premiere or is near completion and, depending on the outcome, may not need one.

A sales company represents you and your film while seeking the best distribution deal. They work with filmmakers to build their marketing strategy and deliver the essential elements needed to attach a distributor.

Films are sold by territories or by country. Some or all rights are sold to distributors in each territory, including: theatrical, online – VOD + SVOD, AVOD, TVOD, etc., DVD (less so), PPV (pay-per-view), free TV, airlines.

As I have said before, a producer sells rights in the film to raise money or make money back – these rights are the right to distribute and the right to exhibit the film.

> VOD = Video on Demand
> SVOD = Subscription VOD
> AVOD = Ad-based VOD (YouTube)
> TVOD = Transactional VOD (pay based on the amount you watch)

A sales agent can sell the film either before it is made (pre-sales) or at any stage during post or after completion. Pre-selling and minimum guarantees (MGs) are other, less likely, ways of raising money towards the film's budget. Let's face it, though – in today's climate, getting a minimum guarantee is extremely rare and the exception to the rule.

It is also worth noting that until the film has become profitable, and the distributor and sales agent recouped their expenses, the filmmaker won't see a profit. Usually there is a collection agency management agreement in place where a collection agent will collect and distribute all revenues.

PETER SMYTH: Really target distributors and sales agents at script stage. They're unlikely to pay an MG at script stage for a low-budget film but they will indicate if they are interested or not and can then provide guidance on script, casting, etc. If you struggle getting a sales agent or distributor on board at script stage, you will struggle more once the film is finished. And it's much easier to change a script to make it sellable than it is to change a finished film.

WHAT DO SALES COMPANIES DO?

A sales agent is a person or company with great connections in film sales across the globe – they divide the world into territories (countries). It is through their connection with buyers that they sell your films. They get to know the needs and wants of each territory and much of their business has been done in film markets.

I personally believe that approaching a sales agent can help you improve your project as they can tell you what works and what doesn't from a purely commercial perspective. That said, it's rare to get a sales agent on board before a film has been to a festival or created a buzz.

They can guide a project in terms of market and audience and often provide sales estimates which are useful as many financial investors will request sales estimates or that a sales company is attached before they invest in the film, as they are looking for a viable entity.

While it is rare to get them on board early on, they are all supporters of new talent and independent films, and they really know their

COLLECTION ACCOUNT:

You may need to share revenues from a production with financiers, production partners and/or talent OR you may be entitled to a pre-agreed share from a production's revenues.

A collection account management (CAM) can securely and visibly collect, manage and pay out revenues for you.

The money the film makes is placed in a safe, unlikely to go bankrupt, remote-collection account.

markets. If you get to know a sales company, they can give you solid feedback on your work. In my early days I didn't understand what they did. To get the most from this I approached four people whose knowledge of sales has helped me personally or my projects.

BRIAN O'SHEA: We act as a representative of a film and sell the distribution rights to a specified territory (domestic or international) on behalf of the filmmakers. The sales agent makes a fee based on all gross receipts accumulated as a result of the agent's sales.

HILARY DAVIS: A sales company is the link between the creatives (producers/writers/directors) and the festival selectors and buyers who will eventually handle your film. It's very hard to operate without a sales company on board to guide you through the whole process.

CLARE CREAN: Primarily, a sales agent is the link between the independent production and worldwide distribution. The majority of sales agents have hundreds of distribution contacts throughout the world and a good sales agent will know his or her buyers well enough to know the type of films they acquire. The sales agent will provide an estimate of a film's value worldwide and many sales agents provide a contribution to the financing of a project, either in the form of a sales advance or in pre-sales.

SARAH ARNOTT: A sales company will license rights to your movie in the international marketplace at various stages (from script to screen). They are usually the piece of the puzzle that triggers the financing and are therefore a crucial part of the process. A good sales agent is the bridge between the creative and the financial, guiding producers through the festival and distribution process.

WHAT SHOULD A FILMMAKER SEND YOU?

BRIAN O'SHEA: Sales agents look at a number of elements when evaluating a project. If the project has not been shot yet, a final draft of the script is appropriate. Any information on the director (and his/her past credits), cast, and the producer(s) is also helpful. We are basically looking for what can be used as good selling points. It helps tremendously when a filmmaker has already thought of this and highlighted these selling points in the submission.

HILARY DAVIS: Look book, script, all production details, finance plan.

CLARE CREAN: The most useful tool for any sales agent is a really decent synopsis. Most sales agents can form an opinion on the viability of a project on the synopsis alone. In addition to the synopsis, a script, cast and crew list, budget/finance plan, and some information on the shoot. Links to the director's previous work (especially for first-timers) are always useful but filmmakers don't need to go to the expense of creating an entire marketing campaign.

WHEN DO SALES GET INVOLVED?

CLARE CREAN: The answer to this question really rather depends on what stage you are at with your project and what it is you require the agent to do. If seeking a contribution to financing, bring us on board as soon as possible. We will want to be involved in the creative/talent decision-making process. In the current climate, pre-sales will require a certain level of casting and a known director attached. A script should be as close to fully developed as possible. The agent will need to see the finance plan, the budget and full details of all other financiers. If the project is fully financed, a producer should present the complete package. The script should be fully developed, with director and cast, etc. all confirmed. This is often not the type of project to be pre-sold – maybe it's a first-time director or unknown cast – but the sooner an agent can begin to raise buyer awareness of the project the better.

HILARY DAVIS: At an increasingly early stage, as the really good scripts disappear off the market quickly – this is a major change for sales companies and, unless you have access to finance, it's very hard to survive on sales commissions and fees these days.

SARAH ARNOTT: Various stages – from script to finished film. However, it is increasingly important to get involved as soon as possible – sales companies know the best projects get snapped up early.

BRIAN O'SHEA: Sales agents get with a project at every stage, as long as there is material to evaluate.

SAMPLE SALES ESTIMATES

A sales estimate will be a full document showing what the agent thinks each territory is worth. It lists all the major countries (known as territories) and the maximum price achievable. At the end they will total it and tell you what they estimate will be the total yield from the film worldwide. I've listed a few countries here to demonstrate, but a proper sales estimate would list all the territories in the world.

These estimates are only meant to demonstrate what the figures would look like and should not be taken as a given for any film. Only dependable and established sales companies or distribution professionals can create estimates for a project, and they are based on changeable factors such as the people involved in the project, the market, box-office performances, etc.

All quoted prices are in $000s	Max	Probable	Minimum
France	10	7	5
Germany	12	9	7
Greece	9	5	5
Iceland	9	6	3

ROCLIFFE NOTES on...

SALES AGREEMENTS

- A sales company will present you with a sales estimates sheet showing you the asks (which means the price they will ask for).

- Always have a film lawyer look over any agreement.

- If you have been offered pre-sales or an MG, ask for proof of the sale that was made and the payment dates to the sales agent and potentially to you.

- Reserve rights on novel, publishing (music and electronic), soundtrack, merchandising, TV production, interactive.

- Ensure an agreement lists meaningful consultation not approval on cast.

- Define and cap market fees, distribution and sales costs.

- Recoupment schedule to be clear, including deferrals.

- Direct distributor to pay all gross receipts into the collection account without cross-collateralisation.

- List what the essential elements are.

- Request a long-form standard T&C, including info on default or accounting.

- Keep informed of festivals and all sales from markets.

- Negotiate the deliverables – for example, is a 35mm print still needed?

WHAT ARE THE BENEFITS OF HAVING SALES ON BOARD?

SARAH ARNOTT: Understanding the timing of the presentation of a project to the market – we are constantly talking to international distributors; however, it is still important to launch a movie at a major market/festival. We will also give you 'market' information re: budgets, cast, etc.

CLARE CREAN: Filmmakers often feel that the role of a sales agent is solely that of the party that brokers a deal. This couldn't be further from the truth and the smart producer understands that the sales agent works in conjunction with the filmmaking team to ensure the success of a film. Agents can provide a producer with a knowledge of the worldwide market and give advice on what films sell well and, perhaps more importantly, what films don't. The sales agent will provide an estimate of a film's value worldwide, which is often the key to a producer unlocking finance for their film. Most sales companies will provide expertise in marketing and promotion. The sales agent will often create an initial marketing campaign for a film and help filmmakers in producing artwork, trailers, etc. The sales agent will be able to advise on the best strategy for the film. Should it be submitted to certain festivals, at what point should the film be screened for buyers, and what is the best way to generate press? In addition to contracting and delivery for every deal that is concluded, the sales agent will work closely with the local distributor on their release strategy and marketing campaign. Once a deal has been concluded, the most successful films might continue to generate revenue for years. It is the job of the sales agent to continue to collect all outstanding revenue.

BRIAN O'SHEA: A sales agent can advise on which elements have value, thereby allowing you to package a valuable film. Sales agents can also close pre-sales, which help finance the production of the project. Lastly, sales agents can gauge distributors' appetite for a project before any major decisions on rewrites, shooting and packaging are made.

HILARY DAVIS: They guide the film at every step of the way, from introducing the script to buyers before it is made to presenting the finished film at its launch festival.

ADVICE FOR CREATIVES?

SARAH ARNOTT: Plan ahead – scripts pitched in the days before (or during) a market won't get much attention. Be clear about where you think the script sits – is it ready to go or does it need further development? Partner with a sales company that shares your vision for the movie and will pitch it accordingly to distributors. Think about how you would position the movie – it helps if the company believes you also understand who your movie is for and that you're thinking about its release.

CLARE CREAN: Do not cut corners on stills photography and/or extras. Brochures, artwork, publicity materials will all need to be created, whether they are for the sales agent or local distributor. It is impossible to create decent publicity materials without decent photography. Most sales companies will have a submissions policy. Check out the company website before sending an unsolicited project. Sales companies rarely take unsolicited meetings with producers at markets. Do not attempt to meet a sales person in Cannes or Berlin without having had any prior communication.

BRIAN O'SHEA: The most important advice for filmmakers is something they probably get from every other industry professional: make your project unrejectable. Sales agents are constantly looking for reasons not to get involved with a project, so make it so they can't stop thinking about what you've sent. This means really honing the script, because everything will come together with a great, compelling, well-written narrative.

HILARY DAVIS: Know what you have in terms of genre and what you want to achieve. Know your audience and think ahead beyond production to the launch and eventual distribution of your film.

DIRECT OR SELF-DISTRIBUTION

The secret is knowing who your audience is and how you're going to reach them.

A film may have a niche audience, but many of us know little or nothing about connecting with that audience. Most filmmakers find themselves with this dilemma, usually after the film has been made. Most see themselves as creatives whose job it is to raise the money and tell a good story, after which the film will get picked up.

Many films in the indie sector are self-financed or crowd financed. Others have availed themselves of the soft-funding ventures. Either way, you want an audience to see the film.

Sign up to Stephen Follows' blog (www.stephenfollows.com) as he publishes weekly research projects on all aspects of the film industry. He offers some of the most informative, data-driven analysis of the film industry and has been commissioned to write reports for key film-industry bodies, his most recent study having looked at gender inequity in the UK film industry. Read the BFI reports, too, and look up research published by Olsberg Spi (www.o-spi.co.uk). Track the box office and look back at box-office history at sites like Box-office Mojo, Screen Daily, IMDb and Charles Gant's column in the *Telegraph*.

JONNY PATERSON: The cost of getting to markets and making the most of them has been a little out of my reach thus far. That said, one of my first jobs in entertainment was working at Lionsgate and, during my tenure there, I became a big fan of AFM (American Film Market), which takes place in Santa Monica each year. There are a lot of filmmakers, producers, financiers, etc., in town for this event and, although I wouldn't attend with grand expectations of pitching to the likes of Lionsgate, as they go there with very specific mandates and have their time pretty meticulously scheduled in advance of the first day, I believe there is a lot to be said for attending and seeking out like-minded filmmakers who could ultimately be collaborators.

CHRISTINE HARTLAND: A big learning curve for me was feature-film distribution, as the industry was being disrupted with technology and new distribution models. I realised very quickly that we needed to make as much noise as possible for the film industry to notice us and also for the audience to discover our film. *WMD* was one of the first British films to follow the reverse distribution strategy and have a simultaneous iTunes and limited theatrical release in the UK in 2009.

HELEN SIMMONS: When I realised we needed to self-distribute *Chubby Funny*, I initially felt absolutely overwhelmed. We had a film every sales agent and distributor we'd met had claimed to adore, but none of them knew how to sell it. How was I – a complete newbie – meant to find an audience? The first and most crucial thing I did was ask questions. I sought out producers who'd done the same, I read articles, I contacted friends in the industry for very specific bits of knowledge. I contacted boutique companies that could help us through the journey, and weighed up the pros and cons of using them versus going it alone. Eventually, I found a wonderful cinema booker who agreed to come on to the film because he liked it, and we did a deal where we'd split any theatrical profits so I didn't have to pay money I didn't have up front. I contacted some publicists and showed them the film, and one of them loved it so much they agreed to give me some emails and send the film to influential people and journalists. I contacted film reviewers on Twitter and tried to sell the film as best I could and make them watch it. Once they'd seen it, those that enjoyed it went out of their way to support us, and it really gave me faith in the whole process. After reluctantly agreeing to screen us, cinemas saw that people were actually buying tickets, and we ended up in cinemas across the UK for just under four months. Social media was my best friend – we planned tweets and Facebook posts and Instagrams religiously, and tried to spread the word through every avenue we could. Word of mouth was the best way of getting bums on seats. It was hard work, but nowhere near as hard as I'd feared, and we ended up making more money than a few indie films that year that had starry names and a proper distributor behind them.

DOMINIC BUCHANAN: Understand that, for low-budget films, theatrical is not king.

••

A ROCLIFFE CONVERSATION with
CHARLES GANT

Charles Gant is Features Editor at *Screen International* and has a weekly column that looks at how the UK box office has performed on a weekly basis. It is essential reading.

FA: Is the UK unusual in that we share a dominant language?

CG: Yes, the UK is relatively unusual in that we share a language with the dominant supplier of film and television – North America – which is a challenge but also provides more chances for exporting your films. Unlike every other European country except Ireland, making films in the English language doesn't give them a USP. UK audiences are in no danger of being deprived of films in their own language. So that is a challenge for domestic production. It's also an opportunity, since your chances of exporting are also greater. English is the first or second language for most of the world. When budgeting a film you must decide: are we seeking to recoup out of the UK, or does this have international appeal? Cinema admissions have gone up from 1984 at 54 million to 172 million in 2015. And they edged back to 168 million in 2016, but have basically tripled since the low point of the mid-1980s and a record-setting 2017.

FA: Is the reason because the product has changed?

CG: Not really. The turnaround began with the building of multiplexes. There has been a revolution in the UK cinema-estate portfolio since the 1980s. From the 1960s, there was a chronic lack of investment in cinemas. That has all changed and investment is ongoing. And as audiences started to increase globally, Hollywood has had an incentive to make more and bigger blockbusters, which are now regularly released throughout the 12-month calendar, not just summer and Christmas time.

FA: There has been a steady rise in UK films.

CG: True. In the early 1990s, look at the annual top-twenty lists for the UK box office, and you will look in vain for a British film. *Four Weddings and a Funeral* was the beginning of the change, then *The Full Monty*, then Working Title as a regular supplier of commercially ambitious films, the reinvention of Bond with Daniel Craig, Harry Potter films and more. At the more indie end of the scale, Channel 4 and Film4 were important, then the creation of the UK Film Council.

FA: Digital has changed the landscape because we can now programme more films.

CG: Yes, and the number of cinema releases each week has expanded. But audiences' time doesn't magically expand, it is finite, and in fact entertainment options proliferate.

FA: Is it essential to know what different audiences like?

CG: Yes, but you can't second-guess the market. Still, understanding audience trends doesn't hurt, and knowledge of the marketplace might help in pitch meetings. It's respectful to financiers to know about the marketplace, as it suggests you care about the commercial outcome of the film.

FA: Is it easier to pinpoint what the older or upscale audience want, like period films or literary adaptations?

CG: This is a simplification, but it is true that there are a number of specific challenges with other genres within British film (thrillers, comedies, romcoms, family films), and we do tend to make prestige dramas well in the UK, often set in the past, often based on literary source material. And they do export. For this older audience, it's hard to fail with Maggie Smith, Judi Dench, Helen Mirren, etc., but also hard to succeed without an actor who is meaningful to them, and it's quite a short list.

FA: It is perceived that auteurs play at festivals – they travel, they do well around the world?

CG: Not 'do well', but they do sell around the world. And film finance isn't purely market-driven. The BFI, and also Film4 and BBC Films, are not indifferent to commercial success – it's great when a *Lady Macbeth* comes along and connects with audiences – but there are plenty of British auteurs who continue to receive backing despite consistently delivering only modest box office. If the film plays in prestige film festivals and wins awards, the broadcasters and BFI and other sources of soft money might overlook some red ink on the balance sheet.

FA: Does documentary have the potential to have a special-event premiere?

CG: It depends on the film: who would the Q&A be with, and would people pay for that? Music docs are a rich area with which to create event presentations, and so can political docs be.

....

WHAT ARE AGGREGATORS?

I discovered there are companies who can help you get your film online. I spoke to Andrew Nerger from The Movie Partnership about what they do.

ANDREW NERGER: As aggregators, we are approved agents for several online platforms as we know the legal, technical and infrastructure needed to place films. It costs money to upload films on to platforms so how we work is by charging up-front fees or a percentage to encode and upload. Over the years we've become more selective in what we take. As we've come to know what the anticipated demand estimates can be, we might sometimes advise filmmakers to go directly to Vimeo or Amazon on demand as we can tell if a film is too indie or they won't have the resources to create an online marketing or social-media strategy. It is fine to go straight to Amazon and select Amazon Prime and US. Often what's holding filmmakers back is their own expectation of the film doing a theatrical or platform release on Netflix. That isn't often a given with films. You need to be smart about this because, on Amazon or iTunes, the reality is that you're up against big films with massive campaigns and reviews behind them. When a film has a good review or some form of buzz, such as a BAFTA nomination, that helps, but the punter on VOD doesn't necessarily read these reviews, so you have to think outside the box. We will discuss with a filmmaker their options, such as potential sales to a broadcaster, but we tend to be very realistic about expectations, both for them and for us. It has to work both ways. The films I see doing best are ones with a compelling title, smart artwork and a good social-media strategy.

ROCLIFFE NOTES on...

DIRECT OR SELF-DISTRIBUTION

- Self-distribution takes an **enormous** amount of work and effort – as much as getting a film financed and made. Save some of that energy for the distribution if this is the route you want to go down.

- You need to think about this at the beginning of the life of a film, even for investors.

- Bring in a publicist months, not weeks, beforehand to start creating press and content around the film and planning how that content will be used.

- Your artwork and trailer are essential and should be done by professionals – this is how the film is first perceived.

- Get your film on the festival circuit as this generates interest and reviews – hopefully positive ones.

- Find out about your local or indie cinemas and who runs them. Otherwise you have to ring every cinema chain to get them to book your film.

- Some indie cinema chains will ask you to provide a marketing and release strategy or plan to show how you will attract an audience.

- Aggregators such as The Movie Partnership (www. themoviepartnership.com) and Under the Milky Way (us. underthemilkyway.com) can help pave the way for online platforms as they are respected providers.

- You can put your film on iTunes yourself but it's time-consuming.

- Work with consultants like Miracle, Andrew Woodyatt, David Shear at Shear Entertainment, The Film Collaborative, Deborah Rowland at We Are the Tonic or Ava duVernay's Array.

- Consider hiring a cinema booker.

- Contact airline programmers and broadcasters to do deals directly.

- Identify who your niche audience is as they are the ones who will pay to see your film and spread the word about it.

- Create a range of products to advance the film – community screening licences, educational licences, discussion sheets, DVDs.

- Look at what you are up against in terms of other film releases and time of year.

....

PAUL SNG ON MAKING, MARKETING AND DISTRIBUTING *DISPOSSESSION*

I made *Dispossession: The Great Social Housing Swindle* to explore the neglect, demolition and regeneration of council estates across the UK, and reveal the impact of the housing crisis on working-class communities in Glasgow, London and Nottingham. As well as writing and directing the film, I was the sole producer, and thus responsible for every aspect of the production, from financing the project through to the basic admin. I also self-distributed and managed the marketing.

The film was released five days before the terrible events of the Grenfell fire, which made our subject matter grimly relevant. I knew we needed to be respectful and sensitive to the people who'd lost their lives and their families, but also that the neglect and mismanagement of council and social housing in the film deserved wider attention.

The financial challenges involved in producing and self-distributing this film were immense: a micro-budget of £35,000 for filming, editing and post-production, and £10,000 to cover marketing and distribution costs. And yet we have put the film on more than 120 screens to date, selling out screenings across the UK and receiving plaudits from Kate Muir in *The Times*, Michael Sheen, Rebecca O'Brien and Jeremy Corbyn, and strong reviews in the *Big Issue*, the *Guardian*, the *Observer*, *New Statesman* and many more.

As a result, I decided to run a campaign in tandem with the film that would promote grassroots housing campaigns and explore alternative solutions to estate demolition. I added a section to our website that listed a number of groups from around the country and invited local campaigners, housing-sector workers and politicians to each of our Q&A screenings, to encourage debate and promote actions in the areas where the film toured. The film has grossed over £73,000 in box-office receipts to date and was released by Verve on home entertainment in late October 2017.

I've overseen the whole process with a small, trusty team and attended most of the Q&A screening events to date, sharing a platform with brilliant speakers such as Jeremy Corbyn, Ken Loach, Caroline Lucas, Michael Sheen and many of the people who appear in the film. I felt it was essential to give this film over to the people who are affected by the issues discussed in it, and we are currently arranging free screenings for people on estates and in local communities.

I'm often told I should be proud of the film; pride somehow doesn't seem appropriate when thinking about the people who have lost or are fighting to save their homes. I hope the film is owned as much by the people affected by this crisis, and that it is helping to raise awareness about what's happening to council estates across the UK, encouraging people to defend their homes from demolition and preserve their communities. Film is a powerful medium, and preserving communities and bringing about social justice through our work is of vital importance to me.

LINDSAY CAMPBELL FROM UNDERGROUND FILMS ON SELF-DISTRIBUTING *ONE MILLION DUBLINERS* AND *STRANGE OCCURRENCES IN A SMALL IRISH VILLAGE*

We got a distribution loan from Screen Ireland for €10,000 (we paid this back). We also engaged a publicity company (who did traditional PR) and contacted all our press contacts. We did social media ourselves on the first film and then hired a digital media consultant for the next.

Contacting 203 cinemas and asking them to take the movie was very time-consuming and took four months.

With the posters and marketing materials, we had someone create these. We had them printed and distributed.

We looked at alternative ways to market the film without paying for massive advertising. For example, the PR company ran a competition in the newspaper offering 50 sets of tickets to the premiere. It was a banner on the front page. So you lose those seats BUT you gain advertising space you could never afford and get the knock-on publicity.

We offered relevant groups like Passport for Leisure a discount initiative for people over the age of 55 and offered them some free tickets, which meant they talked about the film and took people with them.

We were lucky we sold out the Galway Film Fleadh premiere and won the prize in Galway, so we were able to use this on publicity materials.

We had a trailer and four 90-second clips which we released.

We carefully looked at the time of year and avoided clashing with the World Cup, Wimbledon and bank holidays. Note the times of year cinema is slow. We were also mindful not to compete with

Oscar launches from September onwards – although this isn't the worst idea, as it offers alternate viewing.

We did a press screening a week before the release with the publicity company and invited well-known radio presenters and journalists and asked their opinions. We used their comments in the media build. This was cut into the trailer and crested into two-minute stings and posted online.

We split up the multiplex so that six of us asked our respective groups and demographics to go to respective cinemas so they'd be full for opening weekend. It meant our opening weekend had a strategy to it and decent numbers in more than one cinema.

We put flyers in tourist offices and bus depots via their head offices months in advance.

One Million Dubliners was in cinemas for five weeks.

TIPS FROM UNDERGROUND ON SELF-DISTRIBUTION

- Bums on seats are what matter.

- Plan your strategy months in advance.

- Create a distribution document.

- Do a SWOT (strengths, weaknesses, opportunities, threats) analysis.

- Social media and strategy is key.

- Make sure you get the message YOU want to get out.

- A press release must have something to say and direct the journalist, and thereby the reader, to a screening and be very clear when the film is on and in which cinemas.

- With niche audiences, tell them why they should be interested.

- Also identify this audience as you are producing the film. There are lots of interested parties you should be aware of from as early as possible so you can exploit connections as much as possible.

- Slowly drip-feed the social media to keep people interested. We hired a social-media expert to do this as there isn't a real logic to it – a very worthwhile investment.

- Crowdfunding can generate its own audience.

LISTS

This is by no means a definitive list and should serve as a guide.

RECOMMENDED READING

- *Rocliffe Notes: A Professional Approach for Screenwriters & Writer-Directors* by Farah Abushwesha
- *Film Directing Shot by Shot* by Steven D Katz
- *The Guerilla Film Makers Handbook* by Chris Jones & Genevieve Jolliffe
- *How to Audition on Camera* by Sharon Bialy
- *Make-Up is Just Colored Dirt* by Shannon Thompson

DIRECTORIES

BROADCASTERS

ARTE (France)	https://www.arte.tv/en/
BBC Films (UK) *BBC Films does not accept unsolicited scripts. In the first instance, contact BBC Writersroom.*	www.bbc.co.uk/bbcfilms/about
Film4 (UK)	www.channel4.com/commissioning/4producers
RTE (Ireland) *Look under e-commissioning*	https://about.rte.ie/commissioning/

FUNDING BODIES

AUSTRIA	
Österreichisches Filminstitut	www.filminstitut.at/en
BELGIUM	
Centre du Cinéma et de l'Audiovisuel, Wallonia Brussels Federation	www.audiovisuel.cfwb.be
Vlaams Audiovisuel Fonds	www.vaf.be/Taal/EN
BULGARIA	
National Film Centre	www.ncf.bg/
CROATIA	
Croatian Audiovisual Center	www.havc.hr/
CYPRUS	
Cultural Services of the Ministry of Education and Culture	www.moec.gov.cy/en/cultural_services.html
CZECH REPUBLIC	
State Cinematography Fund	www.fondkinematografie.cz
DENMARK	
Danish Film Institute	www.dfi.dk/omdfi/filmaftaler-og-okonomi
ESTONIA	
Estonian Film Institute	www.filmi.ee/en/funding/categories-of-support/script-support
EUROPE	
European Film Agencies	www.efads.eu/members/members.html
FINLAND	
Finnish Film Foundation	www.ses.fi/en/funding/funding/
FRANCE	
Centre National du Cinéma et de l'Image Animée	www.cnc.fr/web/en/funds
GERMANY	
German Federal Film Board	www.ffa.de/foerderungen-und-antraege.html
GREECE	
Greek Film Centre	www.gfc.gr/en/funding/programs.html

HUNGARY	
Hungarian National Film Fund	www.mnf.hu/en/funding
ICELAND	
Iceland Film Centre	www.icelandicfilmcentre.is/funding/
IRELAND	
Arts Council	www.artscouncil.ie/funding
Broadcasting Authority of Ireland	www.bai.ie/en/broadcasting/funding-development-3/
Department Arts, Heritage and the Gaeltacht	www.chg.gov.ie/arts/creative-arts/grants-and-funding/
Irish Funding	*You can send an email to artscapitalunit@chg.gov.ie*
Screen Ireland	www.screenireland.ie/funding
ITALY	
Directorate General for Cinema of the Italian Ministry of Cultural Heritage, Activities and Tourism	www.cinema.beniculturali.it/
LATVIA	
National Film Centre	www.nkc.gov.lv/en/
LITHUANIA	
Lithuanian Film Centre	www.lkc.lt/en/
LUXEMBOURG	
Film Fund Luxembourg	www.filmfund.lu/
MALTA	
Malta Film Commission	www.maltafilmcommission.com/malta-film-fund/
NETHERLANDS	
Netherlands Film Fund	www.filmfonds.nl
NORWAY	
Norwegian Film Institute	www.nfi.no/eng/grantsfunding
POLAND	
Polish Film Institute	www.en.pisf.pl/funding
PORTUGAL	
Film and Audiovisual Institute	www.ica-ip.pt/en/

ROMANIA	
Romanian National Film Center	www.cnc.gov.ro/?page_id=52953
SLOVAKIA	
Slovak Audiovisual Fund	www.avf.sk/support.aspx
SPAIN	
Institute of Cinematography and Audiovisual Arts	www.culturaydeporte.gob.es/cultura-mecd/en/areas-cultura/cine/informacion-servicios/sc.html
SWEDEN	
Swedish Film Institute	www.filminstitutet.se/en/funding/funding-from-the-swedish-film-institute
SWITZERLAND	
Swiss Federal Office of Culture – Cinema Section	www.bak.admin.ch/bak/en/home.html
UK	
BFI – British Film Institute	www.bfi.org.uk/supporting-uk-film/film-fund
Creative England	www.creativeengland.co.uk
Creative England Fund	www.creativeengland.co.uk/film-and-tv
Creative Europe Desk UK	www.creativeeuropeuk.eu/funding-opportunities
Creative Scotland	www.creativescotland.com/funding
Ffilm Cymru Wales	www.ffilmcymruwales.com/index.php/en/see-welsh-film/funding
Film Agency Wales	www.ffilmcymruwales.com
Film London	www.filmlondon.org.uk/industry
Glasgow Film Office	www.glasgowfilm.com
iFeatures	www.ifeatures.co.uk
Northern Film & Media	www.northernmedia.org/funding/film-tv-development-fund/
Northern Ireland Screen	www.northernirelandscreen.co.uk
Scottish Screen	www.screen.scot/funding-and-support
Screen South	www.screensouth.org
Screen Yorkshire	www.screenyorkshire.co.uk
Wellcome Trust	www.wellcome.ac.uk/funding

GUILD

Production Guild	www.productionguild.com/
Writers' Guild of Great Britain *WGGB is the union for writers in the UK*	www.writersguild.org.uk

MAILING LIST

Mandy	www.mandy.com
Shooting People	www.shootingpeople.org

MARKETS

American Film Market (AFM)	www.americanfilmmarket.com/
Where: Santa Monica, CA	*When: November*
CineMart	www.iffr.com/en/iffr-industry/cinemart/about-cinemart
Where: Rotterdam, Netherlands	*When: January*
European Film Market	www.iffr.com/en/iffr-industry/cinemart/about-cinemart
Where: Berlin, Germany	*When: February*
Galway Film Fleadh	www.galwayfilmfleadh.com/
Where: Galway, Ireland	*When: July*
Hong Kong International Film & TV Market (FILMART)	www.hkfilmart.com/
Where: Hong Kong	*When: March*
HotDocs	http://www.hotdocs.ca/conference/market_and_forum/
Where: Toronto, Canada	*When: April/May*
Independent Film Week/Project Forum (formerly known as IFP Market)	www.ifp.org/
Where: New York	*When: September*
Les Arcs	www.lesarcs-filmfest.com/en/industry/coproduction-village
Where: France	*When: December*
London Screenings	www.filmlondon.org.uk/industry/sales
Where: London	*When: June*

Marché du Film (associated with Cannes Film Festival)	www.marchedufilm.com/en/
Where: Cannes, France	When: May
MIPCOM	www.mipcom.com
Where: Cannes, France	When: October
MIPTV	www.miptv.com
Where: Cannes, France	When: April
NATPE	www.natpe.com
Where: Miami, Florida	When: January
Sunny Side of the Doc	www.sunnysideofthedoc.com
Where: La Rochelle, France	When: June
TIFFCOM (Content Market at the Tokyo International Film Festival)	www.tiffcom.jp
Where: Tokyo, Japan	When: October
Vertana	www.ventana-sur.com
Where: Buenos Aires	When: Dececember

NETWORK

BAFTA Network x BAFTA Crew	guru.bafta.org/opportunities

ORGANISATIONS

BFI NETWORK	www.network.bfi.org.uk
British Council	www.film.britishcouncil.org/
Screenskills
National training body for Film and Television	www.screenskills.com
Women in Film and TV UK
Various chapters around the world	www.wftv.org.uk

OTHER SALES AGENTS

Celluloid Dreams (France)	www.celluloid-dreams.com
Cinetic Media	www.cineticmedia.com
Film Nation	www.filmnation.com
Fortitude International	www.fortitudeint.com/

Indie Sales	www.indiesales.eu/
K5	www.k5film.com/
Match Factory	www.the-match-factory.com/
New Europe	www.neweuropefilmsales.com/
QED International	www.qed-i.com
Stray Dogs	www.stray-dogs.biz
Synchronicity Films	www.synchronicityfilms.co.uk
The Exchange	www.theexchange.ws
Voltage Pictures	www.voltagepictures.com
XYZ Films	www.xyzfilms.com

RECRUITMENT AGENCY

| Citizen Media Recruitment
Exclusive, boutique recruitment service for the British film and TV industries. Exec level not crew | www.citizenmediarecruitment.com |

TALENT AGENCIES

Berlin Associates	www.berlinassociates.com
Call Box Diary	www.callboxdiary.com
Calltime	www.calltimecompany.com
Casarotto Ramsay & Associates	www.casarotto.co.uk/clients
Chapters	www.chapterspeople.co.ukcom
Dench Arnold Agency	www.dencharnold.com
Echo Artists	www.echoartists.com
Film Industry Talent	www.filmindustrytalent.com
Gems Agency	www.gemsagency.co.uk
Glorious Talent	www.gloriousmanagement.com
IN.TRIN.SIC	www.intrinsic-london.com
Independent Talent	www.independenttalent.com
Jessica Carney Associates	www.jessicacarneyassociates.co.uk
Lux Artists	www.luxartists.net
MacFarlane Chard Associates	www.macfarlane-chard.co.uk/
McKinney Macartney Management	www.mckinneymacartney.com/

Production Switchboard	www.productionswitchboardmedia.com
Reel Angels *Female film and TV technical crews*	www.reelangels.tv/agency
Sara Putt Associates	www.saraputt.co.uk
Scott Marshall Partners	www.scottmarshall.co.uk
Screen Talent Agency	www.screen-talent.com
Suz Cruz	www.suzcruz.co.uk
TOVS	www.tovs.co.uk
United Agents	www.unitedagents.co.uk
Wizzo & Co	www.wizzoandco.co.uk

UK SALES AGENTS

Altitude Film Sales	www.altitudefilment.com
AMP	www.amp-film.com
Bankside Films	www.bankside-films.com
Carnaby International Sales	www.carnabysales.com
Cornerstone Film	www.cornerstonefilm.com
Dogwoof	www.dogwoof.com
Embankment Films	www.embankmentfilms.com
Evolutionary Films	www.evolutionaryfilms.com
Film Constellation	www.filmconstellation.com/contact
Hanway Films	www.hanwayfilms.com
Independent Film Company	www.independentfilmcompany.com
Jinga	www.jingafilms.com/
Kaleidoscope Film Distribution	www.kaleidoscopefilmdistribution.com
Park Circus	www.parkcircus.com
Parkland	www.parklandpictures.com/
Pathe	www.patheinternational.com/en/ accueil.php
Protagonist Pictures	www.protagonistpictures.com
Rocket Science	www.rocket-science.net/
Salt Films	www.saltfilm.com/
SC Films	www.scfilmsinternational.com/
West End Films	www.westendfilms.com/

UK SCREENING ROOMS

Actors Temple	www.actorstemple.com
	07790 072260
Arthouse Crouch End	www.arthousecrouchend.co.uk
	020 8245 3099
BFI Stephen Street	www.bfi.org.uk/venue-hire/bfi-stephen-street-venue-hire
	020 7957 4777
Birkbeck Cinema	www.bbk.ac.uk/roombookings/audio-visual/cinema
	020 7631 6271
Bulgari Hotel	www.bulgarihotels.com/london
	020 7151 1010
Charlotte Street Hotel	www.firmdalehotels.com/hotels/london/charlotte-street-hotel/screening-room
	020 7287 4434
Close Up	www.closeupfilmcentre.com/venue-hire/
Courthouse Doubletree Hilton Hotel	www.courthouse-hotel.com/
	020 7297 5555
Covent Garden Hotel	www.coventgarden.london/hotels/covent-garden-hotel
	020 7806 1000
Dolby Cinema, Soho Square	www.dolby.com/us/en/professionals/content-creation/screening-rooms/london-screening-room.html
Electric Cinema Shoreditch	www.electriccinema.co.uk/
	020 3376 1777
Empire Cinemas	www.empirecinemas.co.uk/
	020 7534 0820
Heavy Entertainment	www.heavystudios.co.uk/
	020 7494 1000
Mayfair Hotel	www.themayfairhotel.co.uk/
	020 7915 3898
Mondrian London	www.mondrianlondonhotel.com/
	020 3747 1099

One Aldwych	www.onealdwych.com/
	020 7300 0700
One Great George Street	www.onegreatgeorgestreet.com/
	020 7665 2323
Rich Mix	www.richmix.org.uk/
	020 7613 7495
Soho Hotel	www.firmdalehotels.com/hotels/london/the-soho-hotel/screening-rooms/
	020 7559 3000
Soho House	www.sohohouse.com/cinemas
	020 7292 0122
Soho Screening Rooms	www.sohoscreeningrooms.co.uk/
	020 7437 1771
The Hospital Club	www.thehospitalclub.com/
	020 7170 9148
Victoria Curzon	www.curzoncinemas.com/victoria/info
	020 7438 9569
W London Leicester Square	www.everymancinema.com/screen-on-the-green
	020 7290 7294
Wired	http://www.wired.uk.com/
	020 7182 7777
BBFC	www.bbfc.co.uk/industry-services/additional-information/preview-theatre
Everyman Screen on the Green	0871 906 9060

UK UNIONS

BECTU	www.bectu.org.uk

BECTU is the UK's media and entertainment trade union; sectors covered include broadcasting, film, independent production, theatre and the arts, IT and telecoms, live events, leisure and digital media.

EQUITY	www.equity.org.uk

Equity is the trade union for actors, stage managers, stunt artists and models in the UK

PACT	www.pact.co.uk

PACT is the trade association representing the commercial interests of UK independent television, film, digital, children's and animation media companies.

APPENDICES

SAMPLE SHORT-FILM BUDGET – £9,000

FILM TITLE		DATE OF BUDGET
Director:		Name
Producer:		Name
Writer:		Name
Budget Date:		DD-MM-YYYY
Format:		Digital/Film
Shoot:		4 Days
Edit:		10 Days (exc down days for feedback)
Post-production:		10 Weeks
Account	**Category Title**	**Total**
1	Producer	0
2	Director	0
3	Writer	0
4	Cast	0
ABOVE THE LINE		0
5	Crew	0
6	Locations	1200
7	Camera Equipment	300
8	Sound Equipment	300
9	Art Dept & Props	400
10	Costume & Make-up	200
11	Stills	50
12	Petrol & Fares	500
13	Production Costs	400
14	Stock/Hard Drives	300
15	Catering	500
16	Vehicle Hire	300
17	Editing Facilities	200
18	Sound Mix	900
19	Foley/ADR	400
20	Grading	900
21	SFX/VFX	500
22	Music	200
23	Insurance	450
24	Deliverables	300
25	Festivals	300
Total Below the Line		8600
Total Above and Below the Line		8600
CONTINGENCY		400
Grand Total		9000
*All figures quoted are guides only - you must get quotes from suppliers		

SAMPLE SHORT-FILM BUDGET – £850

FILM TITLE		DATE OF BUDGET	
Director:		Name	
Producer:		Name	
Writer:		Name	
Budget Date:		DD-MM-YYYY	
Format:		Digital/Film	
Shoot:		4 Days	
Edit:		10 Days (exc down days for feedback)	
Post-production:		10 Weeks	
Account	**Category Title**	**Total**	
1	Producer		0
2	Director		0
3	Writer		0
4	Cast		0
ABOVE THE LINE			0
5	Crew		0
6	Locations		0
7	Camera Equipment		0
8	Sound Equipment		0
9	Art Dept & Props		100
10	Costume & Make-up		0
11	Stills		0
12	Petrol & Fares		50
13	Production Costs		0
14	Stock/Hard Drives		100
15	Catering		100
16	Vehicle Hire		0
17	Editing Facilities		0
18	Sound Mix		0
19	Foley/ADR		0
20	Grading		0
21	SFX/VFX		0
22	Music		50
23	Insurance		450
24	Deliverables		0
25	Festivals		0
Total Below the Line			850
Total Above and Below the Line			850
Grand Total			850

*All figures quoted are guides only - you must get quotes from suppliers

DAY OUT OF DAYS REPORT FOR CAST MEMBERS

Day Out of Days Report for Cast Members

Day/Month	07/09	08/09	09/09	10/09	11/09	Co.			
Day of Week	Mon	Tue	Wed	Thu	Fri	Travel	Work	Hold	Holiday
Shooting Day	1	2	3	4	5				
1. Laurence Magee		SW	W	W	WF		4		
2. Mickey Magee	SW	W	W	WF			4		
3. Alison		SW	W	W	WF		4		
4. Siobhan		SW	W	WF			3		
7. Sean			SW	WF			2		
6. Pearse			SW	WF			2		
9. Bridie O'Neill			SW	WF			2		
8. Patricia				SW	WF		2		
5. Liam			SW	WF			2		
10. SF woman			SWF				1		
11. Handsome Soldier		SWF					1		

Day Out of Days Report for Cast Members

Day/Month			
Day of Week	Start	Finish	TOTAL
Shooting Day			
1. Laurence Magee	08/09	11/09	4
2. Mickey Magee	07/09	10/09	4
3. Alison	08/09	11/09	4
4. Siobhan	08/09	10/09	3
7. Sean	09/09	10/09	2
6. Pearse	09/09	10/09	2
9. Bridie O'Neill	09/09	10/09	2
8. Patricia	10/09	11/09	2
5. Liam	09/09	10/09	2
10. SF woman	09/09	09/09	1
11. Handsome Soldier	08/09	08/09	1

ONE-LINE SCHEDULE

CAST MEMBERS
1 Laurence Magee
2. Mickey Magee
3. Alison
4. Siobhan

7. Sean
6. Pearse
9. Bridie O'Neill
8. Patricia

5. Liam
10. SF woman
11. Handsome Soldier

"THE PARTY" - SHOOTING SCHEDULE OF 4 SEPTEMBER

PRE-SHOOT MONDAY - CALL 5.30PM

REDUCED UNIT

Sheet #: 18 1/8 pgs	Scenes: 18	EXT	ROADSIDE Day Mickeys lifeless corpse, bullet holes in his back	2

End of Shooting Day 1

SHOOT DAY 1

SUNRISE 06:46 - SUNSET 19:59

UNIT CALL - 10:30

Sheet #: 11 1/8 pgs	Scenes: 11	INT	ALISON'S HOUSE - BEDROOM Morning Laurences eyes snap open, shouts from outside	1, 3
Sheet #: 12 2/8 pgs	Scenes: 12	EXT	BELFAST - STREET Morning A siren splits the air, Laurence runs, his world ripped open	1
Sheet #: 1 5/8 pgs	Scenes: 1	EXT	BELFAST - STREET Day Belfast 1972 - Kids play, Siobhan flirts with a soldier	2, 4, 11
Sheet #: 9 5/8 pgs	Scenes: 9	EXT	STREET/ALISON'S HOUSE Night Laurence walks Alison home, they kiss, she invites him in	1, 3

End of Shooting Day 2

SHOOT DAY 2

SUNRISE 06:48 - SUNSET 19:56

UNIT CALL - 12:30

Sheet #: 19 4/8 pgs	Scenes: 19	EXT	SHOP FRONT - BELFAST Day Laurence at a Sein Fein rally "Join the IRA"	1, 10
UNIT MOVE				
Sheet #: 3 1 2/8 pgs	Scenes: 3	INT	LAURENCE'S HOUSE - KITCHEN Day Mickey enters with a cocky grin, the boys welcome him home	1, 2, 4, 5, 6, 7
Sheet #: 5 1 5/8 pgs	Scenes: 5	INT	LAURENCE'S HOUSE - KITCHEN Evening A knock at the door, Mickey ready to bolt, it's just Bridie	1, 2, 3, 4, 5, 6, 7, 9

Sheet #: 13	Scenes: 13 pt 1	EXT	LAURENCE'S HOUSE - BACKYARD Night	2, 6, 7, 9
4/8 pgs			Mickey & Sean having a piss, a shot rings out, Mickey runs	
Sheet #: 6	Scenes: 6	INT/	LAURENCE'S HOUSE - BACKYARD/KITCHE Night	1, 2, 3, 4, 5, 6, 7, 9
1 3/8 pgs			The girls talk, the boys bullshit, Laurence & Alisons eyes mee	

End of Shooting Day 3

SHOOT DAY 3

SUNRISE 06:49 - 19:54

UNIT CALL - 12:30

Sheet #: 2	Scenes: 2	INT	LAURENCE'S HOUSE - LIVING/HALLWAY Day	1, 2, 4, 8
2 1/8 pgs			The woman is actually Mickey, his Aunt welcomes him home	
Sheet #: 4	Scenes: 4	INT	LAURENCE'S HOUSE - BEDROOM Day	1, 2
7/8 pgs			Mickey changes out of dress, has missed his cousin	
Sheet #: 7	Scenes: 7	INT	LAURENCE'S HOUSE - LIVING ROOM Night	1, 2, 3, 4, 5, 6, 7, 9
5/8 pgs			Everyone is drunk, singing and dancing MONTAGE	
Sheet #: 20	Scenes: 13 pt 2	EXT	LAURENCE'S HOUSE - BACKYARD Night	2, 4, 7
2/8 pgs			Siobhan lies dead, a gunman shoots Sean	
Sheet #: 8	Scenes: 8	INT	LAURENCE'S HOUSE - KITCHEN/HALLWAY Night	1, 2, 3, 4, 5, 6, 7, 9
1 pgs			Alison is leaving, Laurence offers to walk her home	

End of Shooting Day 4

SHOOT DAY 4

SUNRISE 06:51 - SUNSET 19:51

UNIT CALL - 12:00

Sheet #: 14	Scenes: 14	INT	LAURENCE'S HOUSE - HALLWAY Day	1, 8
3/8 pgs			Laurence is stunned, Patricia collapses	
Sheet #: 16	Scenes: 16	INT	LAURENCE'S HOUSE - LIVING ROOM Night	1, 3, 8
3/8 pgs			Mickey is alright "on his way to border"	
Sheet #: 17	Scenes: 17	INT	LAURENCE'S HOUSE - BEDROOM Night	1, 3, 8
2/8 pgs			Laurence can't sleep, the phone rings, it's not good news	
Sheet #: 15	Scenes: 15	INT	LAURENCE'S HOUSE - KITCHEN Evening	1, 8
1/8 pgs			Laurence surveys the carage, Patricia tries to scrub the blood	
Sheet #: 10	Scenes: 10	INT	ALISON'S HOUSE - BEDROOM Night	1, 3
1/8 pgs			Laurence & Alison stumble into bed	

End of Shooting Day 5

EXPANDED SCHEDULE

Shooting Schedule

Scene #: 18

EXT	ROADSIDE	Day	Mickeys lifeless corpse, bullet holes in his back

Cast Members
2. Mickey Magee

Props
Rifles

Wardrobe
Blood stained costume
Costume with bullet holes
Militray uniforms

Makeup/Hair
Pale dead look for Mickey

Scene #: 11, 12, 1, 9

INT	ALISON'S HOUSE - BEDROOM	Morning	Laurences eyes snap open, shouts from outside
EXT	BELFAST - STREET	Morning	A siren splits the air, Laurence runs, his world ripped open
EXT	BELFAST - STREET	Day	open
EXT	STREET/ALISON'S HOUSE	Night	Belfast 1972 - Kids play, Siobhan flirts with a soldier
			Laurence walks Alison home, they kiss, she invites him in

Cast Members
1. Laurence Magee
2. Mickey Magee
3. Alison
4. Siobhan
11. Handsome Soldier

Background Actors
2 Soldiers
2 young girls playing hopscotch
4 Adult Neighbours
4 teens running by
5 boys (8-10) playing football

Vehicles
70's car
British army Saracen
Ambulance

Camera
Steadicam

Wardrobe
Militray uniforms

Makeup/Hair
Wig

Sound
Wildtrack of running feet
Wildtrack of shouts

Set Dressing
Bricks
Broken glass
Debris

Special Equipment
Cherry Picker

Scene #: 19, 3, 5, 13 pt 1, 6

EXT	SHOP FRONT - BELFAST	Day	Laurence at a Sein Fein rally "Join the IRA"
INT	LAURENCE'S HOUSE - KITCHEN	Day	Mickey enters with a cocky grin, the boys welcome him home
INT	LAURENCE'S HOUSE - KITCHEN	Evening	home
EXT	LAURENCE'S HOUSE - BACKYARD	Night	A knock at the door, Mickey ready to bolt, it's just Bridie
INT/EXT	LAURENCE'S HOUSE - BACKYARD/KITCHEN	Night	Mickey & Sean having a piss, a shot rings out, Mickey runs
			The girls talk, the boys bullshit, Laurence & Alisons eyes meet

Shooting Schedule

Cast Members
1. Laurence Magee
2. Mickey Magee
3. Alison
4. Siobhan
7. Sean
6. Pearse
9. Bridie O'Neill
5. Liam
10. SF woman

Background Actors
10 crowd (50-70)
15 crowd (18-25)
15 crowd (30-45)

Props
Beer cans
Cigarettes
Glasses
Loud Hailer
Propaganda Flyers
Radio

Music
70's hits on radio

Sound
Wildtrack of screams
Bridie O.S
Pearse O.S

Art Department
70's Fridge
70's Records
Record player

Set Dressing
Sinn Fein posters
Soap Box/Stage
Tricolor Flag

Scene #: 2, 4, 7, 13 pt 2, 8

INT	LAURENCE'S HOUSE -	Day	The woman is actually Mickey, his Aunt welcomes him
INT	LIVING/HALLWAY	Day	home
INT	LAURENCE'S HOUSE - BEDROOM	Night	Mickey changes out of dress, has missed his cousin
EXT	LAURENCE'S HOUSE - LIVING ROOM	Night	Everyone is drunk, singing and dancing MONTAGE
INT	LAURENCE'S HOUSE - BACKYARD	Night	Siobhan lies dead, a gunman shoots Sean
	LAURENCE'S HOUSE - KITCHEN/HALLWAY		Alison is leaving, Laurence offers to walk her home

Shooting Schedule

Cast Members
1. Laurence Magee
2. Mickey Magee
3. Alison
4. Siobhan
7. Sean
6. Pearse
9. Bridie O'Neill
8. Patricia
5. Liam

Background Actors
Gunman

Props
Beer cans
Cigarettes
Glasses

Special Effects
Muzzle flashs
Squibs

Wardrobe
Alison's coat
Blood stained costume
Costume repeats
Jacket with Bullet hole
Jeans & T-shirt
Mickey's dress
Nurses uniform
Set dressing for chest of drawers

Makeup/Hair
Blood around Siobhan
Bullet wound in neck
Wig

Music
Perry como's "Magic Moments"

Sound
Wildtrack of screams
Wildtrack of singing
Playback

Art Department
70's Fridge
70's Records
Record player

Set Dressing
chest of drawers
Mirror
single bed

Additional Labor
Armourer

Shooting Schedule

Scene #: 14, 16, 17, 15, 10

INT	LAURENCE'S HOUSE - HALLWAY	Day	Laurence is stunned, Patricia collapses
INT	LAURENCE'S HOUSE - LIVING ROOM	Night	Mickey is alright "on his way to border"
INT	LAURENCE'S HOUSE - BEDROOM	Night	Laurence can't sleep, the phone rings, it's not good
INT	LAURENCE'S HOUSE - KITCHEN	Evening	news
INT	ALISON'S HOUSE - BEDROOM	Night	Laurence surveys the carage, Patricia tries to scrub the blood

Cast Members
1. Laurence Magee
3. Alison
8. Patricia

Background Actors
R.U.C Officer

Laurence & Alison stumble into bed

Props
Beer cans
Bucket of water
Cigarettes
Evidence bags
Glasses
scrubbing brush

Camera
Overhead Rig

Wardrobe
RUC uniform

Makeup/Hair
Tear stick

Sound
Wildtrack of Patricia
Phone ringing

Art Department
70's Fridge
70's Records
70's TV
News footage on playback
Record player

Set Dressing
Blood spatter
Broken glass
Bullet holes
Debris
Pools of blood
Window boarded

SAMPLE MICRO-BUDGET FILM

Figures quoted are for demonstration purposes only.
Fees and prices will always fluctuate. Check current National Insurance, national minimum wages, levies fees and rates. Check quotes for insurance, cars, facilities, equipment hire.

Director:
Producer:
Version: Version 01
Date: DD-MMM-YYYY

Shooting days: 15
Locations: City - 10 days, Country - 5 days
1 Company Move day

Script version: Based on 7th Draft dated DD-MMM-YYYY

Acct#	Category Description	Page	Total
1000	Story and Rights	Development		£2,000
1100	Producers		£2,000
1200	Directors		£2,000
1300	Cast		£16,752
	Total Above-The-Line		**£22,752**
1500	Crowd and Extras		£2,270
1600	Production Crew		£12,630
1700	Camera Crew		£8,630
1800	Equipment		£13,327
1900	Wardrobe Crew		£4,440
2000	Makeup and Hairdressing Crew		£3,270
2100	Wardrobe, Hair and Makeup Materials		£1,800
2200	Props		£300
2300	Art Department Crew		£6,530
2400	Art Dept Budget/ Set Construction		£3,500
2500	Grip and Crane		£0
2600	Sound Recording Crew		£3,270
2700	Set Lighting		£3,450
2900	Facilities		£3,874
3000	Consumables		£1,200
3100	Locations		£4,300
3200	Transportation		£10,360
3300	Catering, Hotel and Per Diem		£14,570
	Total Production		**£95,721**
3400	Editing		£3,000
3500	Music		£2,000
3600	Post Production Sound		£0
3700	Post Production Deal All incl.		£10,000
3800	Titles & Opticals		£0
3900	Deliverables		£0
	Total Post Production		**£15,000**
4000	Insurance		£1,365
4100	Publicity		£0
4200	Levies & Audit		£935
4300	Legals		£3,000
4400	General Expenses		£650
	Total Other		**£5,950**
	Contingency : 7.5%		£10,649
	Total Above-The-Line		**£22,752**
	Total Below-The-Line		**£116,671**
	Total Above and Below-The-Line		**£139,423**
	Total Fringes		**£2,565**
	Grand Total		**£152,638**

SAMPLE MICRO-BUDGET FILM

Figures quoted are for demonstration purposes only.
Fees and prices will always fluctuate. Check current National Insurance, national minimum wages, levies fees and rates. Check quotes for insurance, cars, facilities, equipment hire.

Director:
Producer:
Version: Version 01
Date: DD-MMM-YYYY

Shooting days: 15
Locations: City - 10 days, Country - 5 days
1 Company Move day

Script version: Based on 7th Draft dated DD-MMM-YYYY

Acct#	Description	Amt	Units	X	Rate	Sub T	Total
1000 Story and Rights | Development							
1001	Writer Fee						
	Writer Name	1		1	2,000	2,000	
	Total						£2,000
1002	Story Rights						£0
1003	Script Registration						£0
1004	Copyright						£0
1005	Supplies						£0
1006	Miscellaneous Development						£0
Account Total for 1000							**£2,000**
1100 Producers							
1101	Producer						
	Producer Name	1	Fee	1	2,000	2,000	
	Total						£2,000
Account Total for 1100							**£2,000**
1200 Directors							
1201	Director						
	Director Name	1	Fee	1	2,000	2,000	
	Total						£2,000
1202	2nd Unit Director						£0
1203	Choreographer						£0
1230	Miscellaneous Expenses						
	Development Expenses						
	Total						£0
Account Total for 1200							**£2,000**
1300 Cast							
1301	Principal Cast						
	1. Character						
	Rehearsals/Fitting	3	Days	1	90	270	
	Shoot Days	15	Days	1	213	3,195	
	ADR						
	Subtotal						£3,465
	2. Character						
	Rehearsals/Fitting	2	Days	1	60	120	
	Shoot Days	15	Days	1	213	3,195	
	ADR						
	Subtotal						£3,315
	3. Character						
	Rehearsals/Fitting	2	Days	1	60	120	
	Shoot Days	15	Days	1	213	3,195	
	ADR						
	Subtotal						£3,315
	4. Character						
	Rehearsals/Fitting	2	Days	1	60	120	
	Shoot Days	5	Days	1	213	1,065	
	ADR						
	Subtotal						£1,185
	5. Character						
	Rehearsals/Fitting	1	Day	1	60	60	
	Shoot Days	3	Days	1	213	639	
	ADR						
	Subtotal						£699
	Total						£11,979

Acct#	Description	Amt	Units	X	Rate	Sub T	Total
1302	Secondary Cast						
	6. Character	2	Days	1	213	426	
	7. Character	2	Days	1	213	426	
	8. Character	1	Day	1	213	213	
	9. Character	1	Day	1	213	213	
	Total						£1,278
1303	Day Players						
	Day Player	3	Session	1	100	300	
	Total						£300
1304	Stunt & Fight Coordinator						£0
1305	Stand-ins						£0
1307	Casting						
	Casting Director						
	Casting Director						
	Casting Expenses						
	Total						£0
1308	Chaperones						
	Chaperone+tutor	15	Days	1	213	3,195	
	Total						£3,195
1330	Miscellaneous Expenses						
	Misc. Expenses						
	Total						£0
Account Total for 1300							£16,752
	Total Above-The-Line						£22,752
1500 Crowd and Extras							
1501	Extras and Crowd						
	Featured extra	1	Fee	2	90	180	
	Featured extra	1	Fee	1	90	90	
	Extras	10	Donation	1	200	2,000	
	Total						£2,270
1502	Stand-ins						£0
1503	Mileage/Car Allowances						£0
1504	Fittings/Interviews						£0
1512	Overtime/Adjustments						£0
Account Total for 1500							£2,270
1600 Production Crew							
1601	Line Producer						
	Prep	15	Days	1	90	1,350	
	Shoot	15	Days	1	100	1,500	
	Wrap	2	Days	1	60	120	
	Subtotal					£2,970	
	Total						£2,970
1602	Production Manager						
	Prep	8	Days	1	90	720	
	Shoot	15	Days	1	100	1,500	
	Subtotal					£2,220	
	Total						£2,220
1603	Production Coordinator						
	Prep	0	Prep	1	90	0	
	Shoot	0	Days	1	100	0	
	Wrap	0	Days	1	60	0	
	Subtotal					£0	
	Total						£0
1608	Location Manager						
	Prep	5	Days	1	90	450	
	Shoot	15	Days	1	100	1,500	
	Subtotal					£1,950	
	Total						£1,950
1604	1st Assistant Director						
	Prep	5	Days	1	90	450	
	Shoot	15	Days	1	100	1,500	
	Subtotal					£1,950	
	Total						£1,950

Acct#	Description	Amt	Units	X	Rate	Sub T	Total
1605	2nd Assistant Director						
	Prep	2	Days	1	90	180	
	Shoot	15	Days	1	100	1,500	
	Subtotal					£1,680	
	Total						£1,680
1606	3rd Assistant Director						
	Shoot	1	Day	1	90	90	
	Subtotal					£90	
	Total						£90
1609	Production Assistant						
	Trainee						
	Total						£0
1610	Production Runner						
	Shoot	15	Days	1	0	0	
	Total						£0
1611	Production Accountant						£0
1612	Script Supervisor						
	Prep	3	Days	1	90	270	
	Shoot	15	Days	1	100	1,500	
	Subtotal					£1,770	
	Total						£1,770
1614	Location Scout						
	Prep						
	Total						£0
Account Total for 1600							**£12,630**
1700	**Camera Crew**						
1701	Director of Photography						
	Prep	5	Days	1	90	450	
	Shoot	15	Days	1	100	1,500	
	Subtotal					£1,950	
	Total						£1,950
1702	1st AC						
	Prep	2	Days	1	90	180	
	Shoot	15	Days	1	100	1,500	
	Subtotal					£1,680	
	Total						£1,680
1703	2nd AC						
	Prep	0	Days	1	90	0	
	Shoot	15	Days	1	100	1,500	
	Subtotal					£1,500	
	Total						£1,500
1704	Trainee						£0
1705	DIT						
	Shoot	15	Days	1	100	1,500	
	Subtotal					£1,500	
	Total						£1,500
Account Total for 1700							**£6,630**
1800	**Equipment**						
1801	Camera Equipment						
	Camera package deal	1	Deal	1	10,000	10,000	
	Total						£10,000
1802	Lighting Equipment						
	Generator	1	Week	1	285	285	
	Total						£285
1803	Sound Equipment						
	Sound Equipment Package	3	Weeks	1	400	1,200	
	Headphone Monitors	1	Week	3	0	0	
	Additional Radio Mics	1	Week	3	0	0	
	Total						£1,200
1804	Walkie Talkies						
	Walkie Talkies+ Earpiece x 24	1	Quote	1	492	492	
	Total						£492

Acct#	Description	Amt	Units	X	Rate	Sub T	Total
1805	Low Loader/A-Frame						£0
1806	Hard Drives						
	Location Hard Drives 3 x 16Tb	3	Units	1	450	1,350	
	Total						£1,350
1807	Stunt Equipment						£0
1808	Miscellaneous Expense						£0
1809	Loss & Damage						£0
Account Total for 1800							**£13,327**
1900	**Wardrobe Crew**						
1901	Costume Designer						
	Prep	10	Days	1	90	900	
	Shoot	15	Days	1	100	1,500	
	Wrap	2	Days	1	60	120	
	Subtotal					£2,520	
	Total						£2,520
1902	Costume Assistant						
	Prep	4	Days	1	90	360	
	Shoot	15	Days	1	100	1,500	
	Returns	1	Day	1	60	60	
	Subtotal					£1,920	
	Total						£1,920
Account Total for 1900							**£4,440**
2000	**Makeup and Hairdressing Crew**						
2001	Hair & Makeup Designer						
	Prep	3	Days	1	90	270	
	Shoot	15	Days	1	100	1,500	
	Subtotal					£1,770	
	Total						£1,770
2002	Hair & Makeup Artist						
	Shoot	15	Days	1	100	1,500	
	Subtotal					£1,500	
	Total						£1,500
2003	Dailies						£0
Account Total for 2000							**£3,270**
2100	**Wardrobe, Hair and Makeup Materials**						
2101	Costumes						
	Costumes	10	Characters	1	100	1,000	
	Miscellaneous	1	Allow	1	500	500	
	Total						£1,500
2102	Hair and Make Up Materials, hair extensions, etc						
	Hair & Makeup	1	Allow	1	300	300	
	Total						£300
Account Total for 2100							**£1,800**
2200	**Props**						
2201	Propmaster						£0
2202	Properties						
	As per Art Department budget						
	Total						£0
2203	Animals						£0
2204	Vehicles						
	Petrol - See main fuel line						
	Total						£0
2205	Loss & Damage						
	Loss & Damages	1	Allow	1	300	300	
	Total						£300
2206	Miscellaneous Expenses						
	Misc. Expenses						
	Total						£0
Account Total for 2200							**£300**

Acct#	Description	Amt	Units	X	Rate	Sub T	Total
2300	**Art Department Crew**						
2301	Production Designer						
	Prep/Wrap	12	Days	1	90	1,080	
	Shoot	15	Days	1	100	1,500	
	Total						£2,580
2302	Art Director/Stby Art Director						
	Prep/Wrap	10	Days	1	90	900	
	Shoot	15	Days	1	100	1,500	
	Total						£2,400
2303	Props						
	Prep	5	Days	1	90	450	
	Shoot	5	Days	1	100	500	
	Total						£950
2305	Art Dept Assistant						£0
2306	Other						
	Painter/decorator	2	Days	1	150	300	
	Graphic designer	2	Days	1	150	300	
	Total						£600
Account Total for 2300							£6,530
2400	**Art Dept Budget/ Set Construction**						
2402	Total Art Department Budget						
	Sets & Props	15	Days	1	200	3,000	
	Total						£3,000
2403	Set Dressing						£0
2404	Strike & Restorations						
		1	Allow	1	300	300	
	Total						£300
2405	Waste Removal						
	Waste Removal	1	Allow	1	200	200	
	Total						£200
2406	Loss & Damages						£0
Account Total for 2400							£3,500
2500	**Grip and Crane**						
Account Total for 2500							£0
2600	**Sound Recording Crew**						
2601	Production Mixer						
	Prep	3	Days	1	90	270	
	Shoot	15	Days	1	100	1,500	
	Total						£1,770
2602	Boom Operator						
	Shoot	15	Days	1	100	1,500	
	Total						£1,500
2603	Addtl Boom Op	0	Days	1	90	0	£0
Account Total for 2600							£3,270
2700	**Set Lighting**						
2701	Gaffer						
	Prep	3	Days	1	90	270	
	Shoot	15	Days	1	100	1,500	
	Total						£1,770
2702	Best Boy/Electrician						
	Prep	1	Day	1	90	90	
	Shoot	15	Days	1	100	1,500	
	Returns	1	Day	1	90	90	
	Total						£1,680
2703	Generator Operators						£0
2704	Electrician						
	Prep	1	Day	0	90	0	
	Shoot	15	Days	0	100	0	
	Wrap	1	Day	0	80	0	

ROCLIFFE NOTES

Acct#	Description	Amt	Units	X	Rate	Sub T	Total
	Total						£0
Account Total for 2700							**£3,450**
2900 Facilities							
2901	Production Office						
	On-site office infrastructure shoot	1	Week	1	100	100	
	Total						£100
2902	Art Department Office						£0
2903	Unit Base						
	Unit base London	1	Allow	1	500	500	
	Total						£500
2904	Rehearsal Space						
	Rehearsal Space - IN KIND						
	Total						£0
2905	Internet. Telephones & Supplies						£0
2906	Equipment Security						
	Equipment security	21	Days	12	12	3,024	
	Total						£3,024
2907	Office supplies						
	Office Supplies	1	Allow	1	250	250	
	Total						£250
2908	Waste Disposal						£0
Account Total for 2900							**£3,874**
3000 Consumables							
3001	Art Department Consumables						
	Allow	1	Allow	1	100	100	
	Total						£100
3002	Camera Department Consumables						
	Allow	1	Allow	1	300	300	
	Total						£300
3003	Lighting Department Consumables						
	Allow	1	Allow	1	600	600	
	Total						£600
3004	Production Department Consumables						£0
3005	Sound Department Consumables						
	Allow	1	Allow	1	100	100	
	Total						£100
3006	Wardrobe, Hair and Make-up Consumables						
	Allow	1	Allow	1	100	100	
	Total						£100
Account Total for 3000							**£1,200**
3100 Locations							
3101	Location Fees						
	Various locations listed	15	Days	1	250	3,750	
	Total						£3,750
3102	Location extras						£0
3103	Location equipment rentals						
	Heaters, Eazy-ups, MUA mirrors, security and production equipment etc.	1	Allow	1	500	500	
	Total						£500
3104	First Aid & Medical Services						
	First Aid Kit	1	Buy	1	50	50	
	Total						£50
Account Total for 3100							**£4,300**
3200 Transportation							
3201	Department Vehicles						
	Lighting truck	1	Rental	1	1,100	1,100	
	Camera & Grip Van	1	Rental	1	800	800	
	Art Department & Props Luton	1	Rental	1	110	110	

Acct#	Description	Amt	Units	X	Rate	Sub T	Total
	Wardrobe van	1	Rental	1	500	500	
	Total						£2,510
3202	Unit Cars						
	Runner cars - hire cars with insurane	15	Days	2	40	1,200	
	Subtotal					£1,200	
	Total						£1,200
3203	Rail Fares						
	Return Trips - Cast	1	Allow	1	500	500	
	Additional	1	Allow	1	100	100	
	Total						£600
3204	Minibus						
	Minibus 16 seater (12hr/day)	15	Days	1	150	2,250	
	Total						£2,250
3206	Fuel & Mileage						
	Fuel	1	Allow	1	2,000	2,000	
	Total						£2,000
3207	Parking, Congestion Charge						
	Parking	1	Allow	1	300	300	
	Total						£300
3208	Additional Travel						
	Train	1	Allow	1	800	800	
	Taxis	1	Allow	1	200	200	
	Total						£1,000
3209	Miscellaneous Expenses						
		1	Allow	1	500	500	
	Total						£500
Account Total for 3200							**£10,360**
3300 Catering, Hotel and Per Diem							
3301	Catering						
	Art Dept prep Sherborne	4	Days	4	20	320	
	London Shoot	35	Persons	10	15	5,250	
	Shoot (3meals/day)	35	Persons	5	18	3,150	
	Subtotal					£8,720	
	Total						£8,720
3303	Accomodation Cast &Crew						
	Cast&Crew Accomodation	5	Days	35	30	5,250	
	Art dept prep Location	1	Allow	1	600	600	
	Total						£5,850
Account Total for 3300							**£14,570**
	Total Production						**£95,721**
3400 Editing							
3401	Edit						
	Shoot to Picture Lock	1	Fee	1	3,000	3,000	
	Total						£3,000
Account Total for 3400							**£3,000**
3500 Music							
3501	Clearances						
	Clearances						
	Total						£0
3502	Song Writers						£0
3503	Composer licence (incl. recording)						
	Composer Buyout	1	Fee	1	2,000	2,000	
	Total						£2,000
3504	Music Supervisor						£0
Account Total for 3500							**£2,000**

Acct#	Description	Amt	Units	X	Rate	Sub T	Total
3600	**Post Production Sound**						
3601	Dubbing Stage						£0
3602	ADR Stage						£0
3603	Foley and EFX Recording						£0
3604	Tape Transfers						£0
3611	Sound Deal inc. Sound Engineer/Designer & Mix						
	Sound Deal						
	Total						£0
Account Total for 3600							£0
3700	**Post Production Deal All incl.**						
3701	Film Leader						£0
3702	Negative Splicing						£0
3703	Picture Reprints						£0
3704	Stock Shots						£0
3705	Opticals						£0
3706	Video Dupes						£0
3707	Video Cassette						£0
3708	Video Delivery						£0
3711	Picture+Sound Post package						
	Picture Deal	1	Allow	1	10,000	10,000	
	Total						£10,000
Account Total for 3700							£10,000
3800	**Titles & Opticals**						
3801	Titles						£0
3802	Main & End Titles						
	Titles - IN KIND						
	Total						£0
3803	Optical Development						£0
Account Total for 3800							£0
3900	**Deliverables**						
3900	Deliverables						£0
Account Total for 3900							£0
	Total Post Production						£15,000
4000	**Insurance**						
4000	Insurance Package						
	Insurance	1	Allow	1	1,200	1,200	
	Insurance tax	1	Allow	1	165	165	
	Total						£1,365
Account Total for 4000							£1,365
4100	**Publicity**						
4101	Publicist						
	Publicist - MARKETING BUDGET						
	Total						£0
4102	Film Festivals						£0
4103	Marketing Materials						£0
4104	Stills Photography						
	Total						£0
Account Total for 4100							£0
4200	**Levies & Audit**						
4201	Skillset Levy						
	0.5% of budget	1	Fee	1	750	750	
	Total						£750

Acct#	Description	Amt	Units	X	Rate	Sub T	Total
4202	Green Screen Levy						
	Green Screen Levy	1	Allow	1	185	185	
	Total						£185
Account Total for 4200							**£935**
4300 Legals							
4301	Legals						
	All Legals	1	Allow	1	3,000	3,000	
	Total						£3,000
Account Total for 4300							**£3,000**
4400 General Expenses							
4401	Health and Safety						
	H&S Policy	Risk Assessment	1	Allow	1	300	300	
	Total						£300
4402	Post Production Script						
	Allow						
	Total						£0
4403	Storage						
	Allow						
	Total						£0
4404	Company Set-up						
		1		1	150	150	
	Total						£150
4405	Miscellaneous Expense						
		1		1	200	200	
	Total						£200
Account Total for 4400							**£650**
	Total Other						**£5,950**
	Contingency : 7.5%						£10,649
	Total Above-The-Line						**£22,752**
	Total Below-The-Line						**£116,671**
	Total Above and Below-The-Line						**£139,423**
	Total Fringes						**£2,565**
	Grand Total						**£152,638**

CONTRACTS GLOSSARY

Compiled by Lee & Thompson, one of the UK's leading law firms for the media, technology and creative industries.

Agreement	Parties	Detail
DEVELOPMENT		
Option and Assignment	(1) Producer (2) Owner	Provides the exclusive option to acquire the rights to a screenplay/ underlying rights (e.g. book or play) to the Producer for a limited time period. If the option is exercised (usually by payment of the purchase price), the rights are assigned and terms such as credits, net profit and future productions become binding on both parties. During the option period, the Producer can develop the project but all rights lapse if the option is not exercised during this period.
Shopping Agreement	(1) Producer (2) Owner/Rights-holder	Allows a producer to be exclusively attached to a project for a set period at no cost, with the intention of the Producer finding parties with the ability to purchase rights and/ or finance the project, but without many of the terms having been agreed. The Producer does not own or control the rights to the project and overall terms must still be agreed between the rights-holder and the Producer.
Treatment Agreement	(1) Producer (2) Writer	For the commission of a writer by a Producer to write a treatment for a film. This will include a provision that the writer assigns the copyright and any other right title and interest to the producer and that the writer will waive all moral rights that the writer may have in the work. There will be remuneration provisions, credits and possibly a first right to write the first draft of the screenplay.

Agreement	Parties	Detail
Interview Agreement/ Contributors Release	(1) Producer (2) Artist/Director	Provides that a party or other contributor providing an interview assigns all rights required, (possibly for an arranged fee). It may also provide for a credit and that the interviewee does not disclose any information related to the film.
Writer's Agreement	(1) Producer (2) Writer	For the commission of a writer by a Producer to create successive drafts of a film screenplay in return for set payments and possibly also a share of budget and/or profits from the film. This agreement assigns or licences the rights in the screenplay to the Producer.
PRODUCTION		
Producer's Agreement	(1) Producer (2) Individual Producer	Provides for the engagement of the individual producer with clauses relating to the services, engagement period, approval/consultation rights, credits and remuneration (budgeted, share of net profits and possibly box office and award bonuses on bigger projects) and other perks (expenses, premiere invitations).
Director's Agreement	(1) Producer (2) Director	Provides for the engagement of the director with clauses relating to the services, engagement period, approval/consultation rights, credits and remuneration (budgeted, share of net profits and possibly box office and award bonuses on bigger projects) other perks (expenses, premiere invitations) and cutting rights.
Actors' Agreement	(1) Producer (2) Artist	Provides for an actor with clauses relating to services, engagement period, approval/consultation rights, credits, remuneration, other perks, promotional obligations and approval over marketing (such as stills).
Crew Agreements	(1) Producer (2) Crew member	Sets out the terms and standard terms on which the people responsible

Agreement	Parties	Detail
		for producing aspects of a film (i.e. those who work behind the camera) are hired, including where their production base is and their specific role, assigning other rights, and setting out remuneration and credits. Often a more detailed agreement is used for a Head of Department (HoD) such as Director of Photography, Costume Designer etc.
Loan Out Agreements	(1) Producer (2) Director/ Producer/ Actor	Provides for the loan of an individual (such as a director, individual producer or actor), under contract with related company to a production company for a specific project. Used as an alternative to a direct appointment of the individual where the individual finds this preferential for tax reasons.
Location Agreements	(1) Producer (2) Location owner	Covers the use of a property/ location by a Producer. Individual terms include insurance liability for breakage and assignment of the right to feature the location in the film.
Composer Agreement	(1) Producer (2) Composer	An agreement between a Producer and a composer for the original score of the film and composition of music together with terms dealing with recording of score, use of composition in connection with film and remuneration.
Musician's Agreement	(1) Producer (2) Musician	Enlists a musician for performance of the original score of the film and composition of music in accordance with the composer's directions.
Stock Footage Agreement	(1) Producer (2) Footage owner	Grants a non-exclusive licence to a production company to include existing footage in a film and to exploit the film containing that footage.
Product Placement Agreement		Grants a non-exclusive licence to a production company to include certain products in a film and to exploit the film containing those products.

Agreement	Parties	Detail
FINANCING		
Collection Account Management Agreement (CAMA)	(1) Collection Agent (2) Sales Agent (3) Investors and Financiers (4) Producer (5) Completion Guarantor (if applicable) (6) Sometimes other parties sharing in net profits	Deals with how all receipts from exploitation of the film (from distributors/broadcasters/other exploiters) are collected and then distributed from a collection account held and managed by a specialist independent collection agent. Includes the definitive "recoupment schedule" which specifies how money in the collection account is to be distributed to the relevant parties such as: Sales agent's fees and expenses, repayments to financiers and investors, deferred cast/crew/producer fees (if any), and shares of net profits.
Completion Bond Agreement (also known as Completion Guarantee)	(1) Completion Guarantor (2) Financiers (3) Producer	Akin to a form of insurance taken out by the Producer with the bond company to ensure completion of the film. Contains two key agreements (sometimes dealt with separately): Firstly the completion guarantor's guarantee to the film's financiers that the film will be finished, and finished on time, otherwise it will repay the financiers' investments. Secondly, an agreement between the guarantor and the producer as to how and when the bond company can monitor and, if necessary, take over production of the film to ensure that it is finished on time.
Executive Producer Agreement	(1) Executive Producer (2) Producer	Governs the services an executive producer provides to the producer. 'Executive producer' (EP) is used as a catch-all title, so terms vary. An EP might be expected to bring finance to the film, so their agreement may include bonuses for money raised. Or they may be an experienced producer/director employed to give guidance to a young creative team, so their agreement might include development days or script reads.

Agreement	Parties	Detail
		Key terms will be the EP's fee, credit, and an assignment of rights.
Financing Agreement	(1) Financier (2) Producer	There are many ways that a film can be financed (e.g. bank loans, grants, purchase of equity shares, the 'discounting' of tax credits) and therefore several different forms of financing agreement. Key terms include: The level of the investment, how and when (or in some cases, if) the investor will get their money back, the rate of interest and/or upfront fee and/or premium being charged (if any), and any other share of contingent compensation (e.g. allocation of "net profits"). Financiers may take security over the rights in the film and/or the assets of the production company (via a security agreement) to secure their investment, and those whose investment is based on promoting a particular country or region will want guarantees of spending in their area. Financiers may also expect a credit and other perks such as approvals over production/sales and invites to set/premieres.
Interparty Agreement (aka Intercreditor Agreement)	(1) Financiers (2) Producer (3) Co-Producers (if any) (4) Production Services Company (if any) (5) Collection Agent (6) Completion Guarantor (7) Sales Agent	Whereas the rights-holding producer generally has individual agreements with the various parties, the IPA governs the relationship between those parties – connecting them all together. The IPA will override all those individual agreements (except the CAMA where their terms conflict) and covers issues such as ensuring all financiers make their funds available at the same time, security (see Financing Agreement), the process for choosing replacement cast or crew and what happens to any underspend or insurance pay out. The IPA will also contain the definitive recoupment schedule, which will be mirrored in the CAMA.

Agreement	Parties	Detail
DISTRIBUTION		
Distribution Agreement	(1) Distributor (2) Producer (Sales Agent may sign on Producer's behalf)	Changing as new platforms appear, but traditionally grants a distributor the exclusive right to distribute the film in a geographical territory for a given number of years. Will also specify which exploitation rights are included e.g. theatrical exhibition (i.e. cinemas), television broadcast, home entertainment (DVD and streaming), and any "ancillary rights" (e.g. soundtrack album sales), and the price, in the form of the minimum guarantee and revenue split, that the distributor will pay. Usually arranged by the sales agent on behalf of the producer.
Exhibitor Agreement	(1) Distributor (2) Exhibitor	Sets out the relationship between a distributor and an exhibitor, i.e. cinema chain, with terms including what percentage of each ticket price the exhibitor can retain and how much goes back to the distributor. May be subject to the approval of the producer. There will be different agreements between the distributor and broadcasters and home entertainment companies.
Sales Agency Agreement		The terms on which the production company engages the sales agent to sell the film as its agent to distributors, including: The agent's commission, agreed expenses, target prices for each territory, and whether the commission is to be deferred (some financiers insist that they recoup their investment in full before the full sales agent's commission is paid).

ROCLIFFE NOTES
A PROFESSIONAL APPROACH FOR SCREENWRITERS & WRITER-DIRECTORS

FARAH ABUSHWESHA

Rocliffe Notes is a compendium for screenwriters and filmmakers which brings together tips and opinions from over 140 film and TV industry professionals, and provides a step-by-step, common-sense guide on how writers and writer-directors can best present themselves to the industry. Including insider insights from award-winning industry players, it details their habits, writing processes, daily passions and preoccupations, whilst also looking at the nuts and bolts of the industry, aiming to motivate writers on their own creative journey, maximise networking opportunities and encourage a professional approach to writing.

An essential armament in any writer's store, contributors include: **Moira Buffini**, **Danny Huston**, **David Parfitt**, **Jack Thorne**, **Sarah Gavron**, **John Madden**, **John Yorke**, **Nik Powell**, **Peter Kosminsky**, **Christine Langan** and **Asif Kapadia**.